Worker-owners: Mondragón revisited

WORKER-OWNERS: MONDRAGÓN REVISITED

A new report on the group of co-operatives
in the Basque provinces of Spain

by

Hans Wiener

with

Robert Oakeshott

a project of the
ANGLO-GERMAN FOUNDATION
FOR THE STUDY OF INDUSTRIAL SOCIETY

The Anglo-German Foundation for the Study of Industrial Society was established by an agreement between the British and German governments after a state visit to Britain by the late President Heinemann, and incorporated by Royal Charter in 1973. Funds were initially provided by the German government; since 1979 both governments have been contributing.

The Foundation aims to contribute to the knowledge and understanding of industrial society in the two countries and to promote contacts between them. It funds selected research projects and conferences on industrial, economic and social subjects designed to be of practical use to policymakers.

© Anglo-German Foundation 1987
ISBN 0 905492 46 3

Printed by George Over Ltd, London and Rugby

Anglo-German Foundation for the Study of Industrial Society
17 Bloomsbury Square   London   WC1A 2LP   Tel: 01 404 3137

Contents

Preface

In 1977 the group of co-operatives based on Mondragón was well established and provided an outstanding demonstration that in the right circumstances and with the right methods this form of enterprise could be entirely successful. But at that time the Mondragón co-operatives were hardly known outside the Basque country, let alone outside Spain. Alastair Campbell and Robert Oakeshott, members of the Industrial Common Ownership Movement, went to investigate, accompanied by Geraldine Norman and Charles Keen as uncommitted observers. The research was financed by the Anglo-German Foundation, which published the result as 'Worker-Owners: the Mondragón Achievement', in the same year.

Much has happened since then: unemployment has come to the top of the political agenda and industrial democracy has gone to the bottom; some co-operatives set up as rescue operations have collapsed; but co-operatives are now viewed with favour as a way of setting up new businesses and creating employment. Moreover, there has been a marked increase in support for the introduction of employee ownership, in partial or more full-blooded forms, into existing businesses. The Mondragón group of co-operatives has become well known. But in response to recession, technological change, and Spain's entry into the European Community, it has greatly changed, and 'Worker-Owners: the Mondragón Achievement' is now out of date.

'Worker-Owners: Mondragón Revisited' is a new report in the same spirit. Robert Oakeshott, who provided most of the background information and the introductions at Mondragón, was a member of the team that produced the first book and has for many years been closely involved with co-operative ideas and their implementation; he now runs a consultancy firm, Job Ownership Limited, which specialises in advising businesses on the introduction of employee ownership. Hans Wiener, who did most of the writing, plays the part of uncommitted observer; as the Anglo-German Foundation's Projects Director he aims to provide readers interested in industrial society in general with a fair appraisal of the importance of co-operatives in the spectrum of enterprise forms. The two share a pragmatic approach; but while this has led Robert Oakeshott to feel cautiously optimistic about the prospects of most kinds of employee ownership, Hans Wiener is not so sure that the idea of the co-operative wholly owned by its workers will spread. Both believe that worker co-operatives can give their members a great deal of satisfaction when they succeed; that they depend on the better side of human nature and that they therefore deserve to succeed; both know that it is not easy, and think it will do society no harm if legislation and taxation are slanted a little in their favour.

Many weightier works have been written about co-operatives in general and the Mondragón Group in particular. The authors do not aim to cover the subject in the same depth, but try to give an overview — a brief history of the evolution over more than thirty years leading to an up-to-date account of the co-operative activity that has spread over much of the Basque country from small beginnings at Mondragón. They report on the changes in Group's structure set in train at the end of 1985 in response to some of the consequences of its growth. And while they do not attempt a great deal of theoretical analysis, they set the Mondragón co-operatives against the background of worker ownership in other forms and in other countries, and hope to provide a perspective on the possibility and problems of this form of enterprise.

London, September 1986

Acknowledgements

We wish to thank all those who have helped us to put this book together. We thank all those who helped to produce its precursor, 'Worker-Owners: the Mondragón Achievement', particularly Charles Nicholson, then British Vice-Consul in Bilbao, who has lent his support ever since, and of course the authors. We are indebted to the Anglo-German Foundation for financing both projects.

We are especially grateful to María Jesús Zabaleta, public relations manager of the Caja Laboral Popular, who organised our visits to Mondragón and spent much time providing us with information and explanations, to Josu Irigoien, head of research, who has been kind enough to provide the figures and other information for our tables, and to Ignacio Mora and others who have checked the whole manuscript for factual accuracy. We thank Roman Balanzategui of Lagun-Aro, Patxi Aldebaldetrecu of Debako, José Luis Jimeez of Nerbion, Victor Saenz of Matrici, Alberto Vidal of Eroski, and all the others who gave their time to guide us through the activities and problems of the subgroups and individual co-operatives. Finally, we acknowledge our great debt to all those behind the scenes on whose written material we have freely drawn, not least the editors and writers of the Group's staff magazine *Trabajo y Unión*.

1 Introduction

Mondragón lies right in the heart of the Basque country, near where the three provinces of the autonomous region meet. The cities of Bilbao in Vizcaya and San Sebastián in Guipúzcoa are on the coastal motorway to the north; Vitoria in the province of Alava, capital of the autonomous region, is in the plain to the south. The country in between is green and mountainous, a land of small hill farms and pastures, winding roads and small old industrial towns. The metal working tradition goes back to the Middle Ages.

Mondragón, which has grown from eight thousand to twenty-seven thousand inhabitants in the last forty years, looks quite prosperous, with much new housing, rather cramped in the valley and spreading up the hillside. And in and around the town it is not difficult to spot factories with the letters S COOP after the firm's name instead of the usual SA of the limited company, for roughly half the working population, about six thousand people, are employed in worker co-operatives.

Altogether some nineteen thousand people now work in well over a hundred industrial and various other kinds of co-operatives in the Group, mostly within a radius of forty miles from Mondragón, some as far as eighty miles away in the province of Navarra. Though not in the autonomous region, Navarra is Basque to some extent, though probably less so than the Basque provinces in neighbouring France. At the centre, at any rate, the Group has a strong feeling of national identity, its annual reports are bilingual and many of its institutions are known by their Basque names; the members' monthly magazine always has pieces in Basque, but it is a moot point whether these are read by members in Bilbao or Vitoria, where the Basques are much diluted by people from other parts of Spain — to Welsh people this will seem quite familiar.

The number of co-operatives has steadily multiplied over thirty years, and during the recent recession hardly any jobs were lost overall because, with sacrifices all round, the more successful co-operatives managed to fit in most of the people displaced from those that had to cut back. This remarkable achievement has attracted world-wide attention, and it is a source of great satisfaction to people who advocate co-operative enterprise, from a variety of motives, as a solution to some of the problems of modern industrial society.

But this is not the success story of industrial co-operatives in general. With thirty years of history behind it, the Mondragón Group — or indeed any enterprise — must be unique. Its success story will not necessarily encourage those who actually wish to set up or join a worker co-operative — it may even suggest to them that in their own circumstances it would be foolhardy to try. The idea of worker ownership is not as simple as it might seem.

Readers who are not familiar with the debate about forms of ownership and control may now wish to turn to Chapter 7, where the various patterns are discussed in more detail. Briefly, the enterprise may be only partly owned by its employees, and it may be owned by only some of its employees — typically by the management and a core group of key workers who have bought the business from the previous owners. Ownership can take the form of individual shareholdings; in employee share ownership schemes of limited companies the shares can be negotiable; in a co-operative there must be rules to ensure that the business does not fall into the hands of outsiders, but the worker members have specific holdings which they can take away when they retire or leave. Alternatively, the holding can be collective; members may have to make a contribution to join, but this is not an investment they can ever withdraw, and the ownership rights come and go with the job. In some forms of collective ownership — such as are usually set up when the original owners of a business make it over to their workforce — the equity is held in trust for the employees, and it is theirs only in the sense that no-one else is entitled to any of the

2

profits and that they are given some powers of control such as voting rights in the election of the Board.

Powers of control can be linked with ownership in different ways or not at all. The ordinary citizen has practically no control over his nationalised industries, and the small shareholder has very little say in the running of a limited company. In West Germany, on the other hand, the co-determination laws give all employees of a company the right to elect a works council, and through it members of the Supervisory Board (*Aufsichtsrat*), though they do not have any kind of title to the capital. In all countries companies involve workers in management decisions through shop floor committees like the currently popular 'quality circles' which originated in Japan. How much say the individual worker really has depends on the extent to which decision making is dispersed and delegated, and it also depends on whether voting rights are related to a person's share in the capital, or to pay grade or rank, or whether everyone simply has one vote.

In the Mondragón Group, the worker members own all the capital, some of it collectively, but well over half in individual shares. They are members of the co-operative in which they work and they each have one vote in the election of its Board; the management is appointed by the Board, but major decisions have to be ratified by the co-operative's general assembly. Nevertheless, they are managed according to strict rules that apply to the whole Group, and they accept a great deal of central control.

Central control of a group of co-operatives presents a dilemma: on the one hand, to ensure the speed of action necessary under competitive conditions, and to achieve economies of scale and the intangible benefits of a corporate identity, there has to be a headquarters organisation with authority comparable to that of the head office of a unified company. On the other hand, the individual co-operatives must remain under the ultimate control of the people who work there and own them; moreover, the people who work in the headquarters organisation should also be members of a co-operative with a capital stake and a vote to go with it. Mondragón's answer is the so-called 'second degree' co-operative, which has other co-operatives as corporate members, and its own workers as individual members. As part-owners of these bodies, the ordinary or first degree co-operatives share in the control of the second degree co-operative by electing their own members to its Board; but they delegate to it — upwards, as it were — the necessary authority to manage. There can be no doubt that the system is effective: the casual visitor to the impressive complex of modern buildings overlooking Mondragón and the surrounding hills cannot but feel that he has come to the head office of a large company. But though only one of the associated co-operatives has ever chosen to do so, they can leave the Group if they wish; and for all the help they may get from the Group, the members are very well aware that in the last resort they are on their own.

The main building is in fact the head office of the Caja Laboral Popular, the Group's bank. The spirit of the whole movement is expressed in its Basque name *Lan Kide Aurrezkia*: *Lan Kide* translates almost exactly into the German *Gemeinwirtschaft* or, roughly, an economy managed in the public interest. The complex includes the jewel in the Group's crown and effectively its head office, the División Empresarial, until recently the bank's management services department. The División Empresarial monitors the performance of all the co-operatives associated with the Group, controls the admission of new ones, and plays the leading part in spotting opportunities and getting new co-operatives set up.

To join the Group, a co-operative must enter into a contract of association similar to the example in Appendix A, which effectively imposes most of the important features of the co-operative's constitution as well as a number of quite onerous conditions, for instance:

- Members of an associated co-operative must put up a substantial individual financial stake, currently about a million pesetas, when they join; they cannot withdraw any of this until they retire or unless they leave and some of it not at all; they may lose it if their business fails.
- Members must agree to put a certain fraction of their co-operative's profits into its general reserve and a further fraction into its social fund before they can allocate any of the profits to increase their individual stakes.
- The associated co-operatives must adopt the Group's common structure for the monthly payments which are to all intents and purposes like wages, but which are called *anticipos* — advance payments — a constant reminder that the money comes out of the members' own pockets. The minimum wage must not be more than fifteen percent above or below the norm laid down

annually by the Caja Laboral, and the maximum must not be more than four and a half times times the minimum (though in some cases top managers have been recruited at higher salaries to work for a co-operative on a consultancy contract basis).

- The co-operative must regularly supply detailed financial information to the División Empresarial and agree to its intervention if things appear to be going wrong.

The organisational structure which cast the Caja Laboral in the role of the Group's head office was the result of evolution rather than design. The bank had been set up because the first co-operatives needed it to harness the savings of an isolated community to help them to grow. The co-operatives were intended to be financed by their members' own capital in the long run, but no business can be run sensibly without using loan capital sometimes — at present about half the co-operatives' capital is represented by loans — and this naturally puts the bank in a dominant position.

The structure served the Group extremely well until quite recently. Now, however, the Caja Laboral has grown to such a size that it has become impracticable to restrict its role to that of the co-operatives' house bank; at the same time the number and geographical spread of the associated co-operatives has made the single-tiered structure rather cumbersome. So it was decided that the time was ripe for major changes. These are the subject of Chapter 3.

The Caja Laboral's own English language publication about the Group is entitled 'The Mondragón Experiment'. This is not meant to suggest that the Group conducts laboratory tests of co-operative practices, but rather that it is forever feeling its way and has no pre-conceived notions about the organisational structures, rules and legal forms it should adopt. Giving the most detailed attention to these, keeping them under review, and not allowing them to ossify is part of the Mondragón tradition, and much of the credit for the Group's success must go to the pioneers, some of whom still hold leading positions today. The new structure may look definitive, but it will surely be only a stage in the Group's evolution.

Don José María Arizmendiarrieta, acknowledged by all to have been the greatest of the pioneers, died in 1976. He more than anyone else thought out the co-operatives' guiding philosophy, the experimental approach and much more besides. His writings are still constantly quoted. He wrote as early as 1963:

'Our strongholds today, the working communities born of the solidarity and unity of those we have chosen to work with, are no longer enough. We must achieve more — unity and solidarity between different working communities, that is to say between a variety of co-operatives. In these days of accelerating economic and structural change the co-operatives' resources and services must be used for a common purpose.'

Thus the idea of a varied but coherent co-operative movement throughout the Basque country has been nurtured from the earliest days. Today the industrial co-operatives in the Group, some of which are described in Chapter 5, range in size from a handful of people to over two thousand, and they engage in activities that range from the very ordinary to the latest high technology. They include agricultural co-operatives, and a retail chain which, by sharing control between consumers and workers, aims to combine the virtues of both forms of co-operative.

Alongside these a great many non-industrial activities have been drawn into the co-operative movement. During the boom period of the early 1970s, housing co-operatives sprang up almost as a matter of course. A much older manifestation of the Mondragón tradition are the educational co-operatives described in Chapter 6: the local technical college founded by Arizmendiarrieta was in a sense the precursor of the first co-operative — the founders had been its pupils. Later many co-operative schools were set up to provide the Basque-medium instruction which had been outlawed under the Franco régime. Now technical education is generally available, and Basque-medium schools are being provided by the state, but much of the Group's research and development effort as well as the recently created management school are in direct line of succession to these earlier ventures.

The Group's health, pensions and unemployment insurance fund (Chapter 4) also has its origins in earlier history. In Spain members of co-operatives count as self-employed, and as the insurance fund available to them at the time was unsatisfactory the Group eventually set up its own system. Though state social security has since become more comprehensive, the co-operatives will stay out of it as far as they can, because their own system is designed in characteristic fashion to reinforce its principles of solidarity. The system has proved inordinately effective in preventing redundancies during the recent recession because it imposes very strict conditions on co-operatives that wish to reduce their workforce and provides various forms of assistance for relocation of people within the Group.

Now that this complex co-operative edifice is firmly in place, Arizmendiarrieta might be asking himself which of its features are merely the scaffolding needed to put it up. Ordinary non-vocational schools are clearly dispensable, and so, probably, are the housing co-operatives; the exclusive social security system may or may not turn out to be essential. The house bank has already ceased to be exclusive, but it is as certain as anything can be that the Group's future development will depend on Caja Laboral finance as it has done in the past. And a form of Group organisation with power delegated to the centre, mutual support of the associated co-operatives, a commitment that the Group's membership should grow and that it certainly should not shrink, a degree of idealism with regard to individual rewards, and a strong sense of Group loyalty — these as well as the bank will surely turn out to be load-bearing structures.

2   Mondragón past and present

Origins

Don José María Arizmendiarrieta, born in Markina in the province of Vizcaya, was a student at a seminary in Vitoria at the outbreak of the Spanish Civil War. He joined the Republican side, worked on Basque trade union newspapers, was captured and very nearly shot. He was eventually released, continued his studies, and was ordained in 1941. His first appointment was in a parish in Mondragón, and so began his association with the town where it was he more than anyone else who provided the inspiration and drive that was to lead to the creation and growth of the co-operatives.

When he first came to Mondragón as a young priest, Arizmendiarrieta was given the special task of looking after its young working people. The main industrial employer in what was then a town of eight thousand inhabitants was the Unión Cerrajera, an iron and steel fabricating business with a large old factory, old-fashioned management and an old trade union tradition. There had been a prolonged strike as far back as 1916, but there were of course no unions under the Franco régime. In 1941, the scene was bleak, and except for a few apprenticeships at the Unión Cerrajera the lack of opportunity for young people was total. Arizmendiarrieta's first achievement was to win community support and to raise funds to set up a technical school. This was opened in 1943 and, to begin with, enabled twenty young men to acquire skilled worker qualifications.

9

The school also provided some general education inspired by Arizmendiarrieta's brand of Basque social Christianity. This could be regarded as the philosophical foundation of the co-operative movement. His concern for education in the community in those early years led to the foundation of the League for Education and Culture in 1948. Later, a whole variety of educational activities developed within the co-operative framework.

But the next and perhaps the greatest step forward was the opening up of opportunities for higher education. In 1947 Arizmendiarrieta managed to persuade the University of Zaragoza to enrol eleven students of the Mondragón technical college in a degree course in engineering, which they would have to take mostly by correspondence and in evening classes. They all passed and graduated in 1952.

Amongst these graduates there were five who had been particularly close to Arizmendiarrieta as students and they now wanted to put his teaching into practice. They first found jobs as junior managers at the Unión Cerrajera, but their attempts to introduce reforms there predictably failed. So they decided to start up an enterprise of their own; Arizmendiarrieta helped them by raising funds in the community — when he put the word around, about a hundred people came forward to put up their money. After a false start trying to revive a bankrupt business in Vitoria, they started from scratch in 1956 and set up ULGOR to manufacture oil-fired cooking stoves in Mondragón. To begin with they merely intended to apply their progressive ideas in managing an ordinary limited company, but after extensive research Arizmendiarrieta pointed them in the direction of a co-operative form.

In 1959, when the legal problems had been sorted out, ULGOR was reconstituted as a co-operative. By that time it had taken over two small foundry companies in a nearby village and branched out into making gas cookers; later refrigerators and washing machines were added to the product range and ULGOR became quite a sizable company; in the days of more labour-intensive production it had a workforce of nearly four thousand, and it is still by far the largest co-operative in the Group. The name ULGOR was made up from the founders' names: Usatorre, Larranaga, Gorroñogoitia, Ormaechea and Ortubay; José María Ormaechea is now the Director General of the Caja Laboral and Alfonso Gorroñogoitia is Chairman of the Board.

The co-operative idea had meanwhile taken root in Mondragón and the nearby villages: five other worker co-operatives had sprung up, as well as a consumer co-operative that was eventually to become the Group's chain of retail stores. But there was not, as yet, a Group. What defined the Group was the association, by contract, of the individual co-operatives with the Caja Laboral Popular.

The Caja Laboral too, was formally launched as a co-operative in 1959. Arizmendiarrieta had persuaded the ULGOR managers to volunteer their services as bankers to the community, at first from makeshift offices, because he had already come to the conclusion that if the fledgling co-operatives were to grow they would need a more solid source of finance than casual borrowing from local people. The lenders too would want the security of a more formal arrangement. Having researched the legislation by which savings banks were then strictly controlled, Arizmendiarrieta had found that a co-operative could have a competitive advantage in attracting funds because it was allowed to offer slightly higher rates of interest; and so it was decided to set up the bank in the legal form of a Co-operative Credit Company.

There never seems to have been any doubt that the co-operatives' capital had to be wholly owned by its workers. It would have been a severe limitation on the wider adoption of this model if there had been no way of borrowing money within the co-operative group. People who wished to set up or join a co-operative had to be able to put up a substantial sum. Only some of them could mobilise enough of their family's savings; the Caja Laboral enabled new members who did not have the money to save it up gradually out of their wages.

The bank also looked after the members' health and pensions insurance. In Spain members of co-operatives count as self-employed, and as such they had to insure with the mutual insurance fund of the self-employed which was not well suited to their needs. The co-operatives' own comprehensive social security system developed by the Caja Laboral, described in more detail in Chapter 4, was separated from the bank in 1967. The system was specially designed to put certain principles of solidarity into effect. Much later, in the recession of the 1980s, the rules relating to transfers of members of one co-operative to another came to assume an important role and helped greatly to avoid redundancies.

The Group's development owes much to the core group of people around Arizmendiarrieta and the Caja Laboral. They were always looking for ways of improving the existing institutions and for opportunities to set up new ones. In 1966, arising out of the educational activities, a unique kind of co-operative, ALECOOP, was set up where students of the technical college could earn their keep through part-time productive work. The research centre IKERLAN was set up in 1977 to develop the high technology necessary to ensure the competitiveness of the products made by the manufacturing co-operatives. The most recent creation is a management training centre, IKASBIDE, set up in 1984.

Growth

Table 2.1 shows how the group grew to its present size from the original four co-operatives associated with the Caja Laboral in 1960. Growth was very rapid in the early years but it continued steadily and just about reached its peak when 'Worker-owners' was written in 1977. The new investment figures show that by 1980 a recession was under way; by 1981 many co-operatives were affected, particularly those in the heavier engineering sectors, with the result that the Group's turnover stagnated and its membership was slightly reduced; 1985 showed a healthy increase in membership and turnover — possibly the beginning of a new phase of growth. How a much worse decline in the early 1980s was prevented is described under the heading 'recession' below.

In addition to the 'industrial' co-operatives counted for the purpose of Table 2.1 the co-operatives associated with the Caja Laboral include seventeen housing co-operatives and nearly fifty schools. Though the League of Education and Culture had been created long before the Group, most of the schools were started in the mid-1970s, and so were the housing co-operatives.

Industrial co-operatives here include agricultural and service co-operatives. Though greatly outnumbered by those in manufacturing industries, they are proof that the Mondragón movement has always been more broadly based. Three of the present nine agricultural co-operatives had joined in the early 1960s; there was then also a fishery co-operative which has not survived. There were five consumer co-operatives in the early days; in 1969 — this explains

Mondragón past and present

Table 2.1   Growth of the Mondragón Group

	Industrial Co-operatives*(+ agricultural coops + service coops)			
year	members	co-ops	sales	new investment in pesetas of 1985[2] (thousand millions)
1960	395	4		
1961	520	12		
1962	801	18		
1963	1,780	29		
1964	2,620	32	–	–
1965	3,441	36	17.5	–
1966	4,202	39	25.1	–
1967	5,082	48	29.3	–
1968	5,981	49	32.3	–
1969	7,945	47	48.4	6.8
1970	8,543	52	50.8	7.1
1971	9,416		54.1	5.3
1972	10,436	57	65.1	4.8
1973	11,417	58	72.6	8.1
1974	12,915	63	83.9	11.2
1975	13,808	65	80.1	11.7
1976	15,417	69	85.6	12.3
1977	16,504	73	94.5	11.0
1978	17,022	78	101.3	8.5
1979	18,295	87	114.2	9.2
1980	18,733	92	119.5	8.2
1981	18,461	89	126.0	7.9
1982	18,788	100	124.8	5.6
1983	18,744	105	128.9	5.7
1984	18,560	111	131.0	7.3
1985	19,200	111	141.0	7.5

* all except educational and housing co-operatives
[2] actual figures adjusted by cost of living index

Source: Caja Laboral

the reduction in the total number of co-operatives in that year — they merged to form EROSKI (see Chapter 5) which has remained a most important constituent of the Group. The service co-operatives too are important; they include of old the Caja Laboral and the social insurance fund Lagun-Aro; but they are also a growth area: engineering design and consultancy co-operatives are among the more recent creations.

After Franco

1976 was a landmark in Spanish history — the end of the Franco era. Through the changes that have since occurred in the political, legal and social background, this has had and is still having a profound effect on the co-operatives.

One such change was the legalisation of trade unions. They have so far made little impact — membership has not grown beyond about 5% of the workforce. As elsewhere, the trade unions are not especially well disposed towards co-operatives in which the workers own and control the capital as individuals; but relations have been quite good and they have not in fact put up any obstacles, though in the big industrial cities where they are much in evidence, particularly in Bilbao, they do not help to create a favourable climate for the spread of co-operatives.

Another important change was the recognition of the national identity of the non-Castilian peoples of Spain. The use of the Basque language in public — banned under Franco — was permitted at once, and a good deal of the central government's authority was devolved, by stages, onto the regions. The Autonomous Region of the Basque Country was set up in 1981. Here Basque is now an official language. Public documents are printed with Basque and Spanish in parallel columns and public notices in Basque abound. On the road to Mondragón some signposts give only its Basque name, Arrasate. The Autonomous Region already provides schools with Basque as the main language, and it seems quite likely that it will eventually make take over most of the co-operative schools. There is no good reason now for a Basque siege mentality, and if the co-operative movement were to rely on this its coherence could be weakened.

For the industrial co-operatives regional autonomy has so far been only to the good. A new Co-operatives Act was passed by the Basque Parliament in 1982. This takes account of the recommendations of the International Co-operative Alliance and partly supersedes the Spanish national legislation, abolishing, for instance, the rule that consumer co-operatives may sell only to their members. The new law owes a great deal to the Mondragón Group, whose role in the history of Basque co-operativism is acknowledged in the preamble, and it is evident that the Group's leaders are not without influence in the regional capital Vitoria. The provision of a Superior Co-operative Council for the Basque Country can be traced back to the co-operative legislation of Catalonia before the Civil War; the Council is the legal successor to any undistributed funds when a co-operative is dissolved. The law also makes provision for a diluted form of membership for inactive 'collaborators'; the intention is to allow people close to the co-operative, particularly retired and other former members, to leave their money invested in it, thus avoiding erosion of the capital base and the total membership but maintaining full employee control.

An area of legislative change that may turn out to be of major importance to the Group is social security: the state system is being extended and the Group's own system must adapt itself to it. Only the pension scheme has been affected so far: members are now insured partly with the the state controlled fund and partly with Lagun-Aro; their combined pension rights remain the same, but they have to pay a little more. They have remained outside the state unemployment system and the co-operatives have declined to take the redundancy payments available under some national and Basque government industry restructuring schemes. The wisdom of going it alone is being questioned, but so far, at any rate, the price of solidarity is being paid and the role of Lagun-Aro has been only marginally eroded.

Economic change

Post-war industrial growth started later in Spain than in most other western European countries. State planning, tariff protection and unsaturated home markets allowed growth to continue when other countries were hit by the oil crisis in 1974, and the full effect of world recession was not felt until later in the decade. Spanish markets have only gradually been opened up to foreign competition, and many tariff barriers are still in place; but they are destined to disappear with Spain's accession to the European Community, and much adjustment will be needed.

The co-operatives were able to grow and multiply as suppliers of both household goods and industrial equipment while the domestic market was still buoyant, but they realised that this could not last and began quite early to build up exports. The value of exports reached 8% of sales in 1969 and 13% in 1972; it fell back to 11% in the mid-1970s and did not rise above 13% again until 1978. But strenuous efforts were made to increase exports when the recession hit the domestic market, and by 1981 exports had risen to their present level of around 23% of sales. The export services formerly provided by the bank have been split off as a separate agency Lankide Export. The Group thus seems well prepared to take advantage of the wider European market, but it will of course be exposed to fierce foreign competition at home.

The overall percentage of exports hides major differences between industry sectors:

Table 2.2   The Group's export sales in 1984

Sector	Pesetas of 1985 (thousand millions)	% of sales
Foundries & forges	4.8	42.4
Industrial plant	5.6	31.3
Machine tools	2.1	26.1
Components	8.2	36.9
Consumer goods	8.1	25.3
Construction	0.8	11.5
Agriculture/food	0.3	11.6
Services	0.1	8.3
Total	30.0	23.0

Source: *Trabajo y Unión*

Recession

The performance of the group in the recession period was a remarkable tribute to the acceptance of discipline in a spirit of solidarity. Redundancies were avoided by a combination of belt-tightening and transfers of members between co-operatives. Volume of output was maintained by accepting sharply reduced margins — in some cases the opportunity was used to build up export markets at zero margins. Members accepted corresponding reductions in real personal incomes. Co-operatives that were still doing relatively well took on, temporarily or permanently, members of those that were hardest hit. Under the Group's rules, a co-operative had to exhaust the possibilities of cutting its own wages before it was allowed to transfer members out. The central organisation acted as labour exchange, and in the last resort transfers could be made compulsory. In all, about 1,500 people were transferred temporarily and 400 permanently. Throughout, the División Empresarial closely monitored the financial performance of all the co-operatives and exercised its powers of intervention when weaknesses of management were detected. The whole complex organisational structure built up over the years had proved itself to the hilt: while most ordinary companies shed labour to maintain their competitiveness — by 1982 unemployment in the region was 16% according to official figures and higher according to the Caja Laboral's own estimates — only about thirty people out of the 18,000 members of the Mondragón Group became wholly dependent on the unemployment fund.

Current problems

Most typical of the people who joined up to form co-operatives in the Mondragón Group's era of growth were the skilled craftsmen and semi-skilled assembly line workers. The level of technology at that time was such that most members could understand all that was done in their enterprise, and the market was receptive if the product was good. But recession and rapid technical change have brought with them the twin imperatives of greater specialisation and improved management performance. The need for qualified staff has always been recognised, and from the earliest days encouragement and assistance has been given to young people to study. Most of these eventually came to work in a co-operative, and at the time this filled the need. But specialisation increased, and not all positions could be filled by local people. In the early 1970s the three-to-one ratio of highest to lowest earnings was relaxed. To a very minor extent it even became necessary to depart from the principle that all workers in a co-operative had to be members, and a small number of specially qualified people had to be employed on contract and paid more than members of equivalent status.

There is also a top management succession problem looming up in the not too distant future. The Group's leadership naturally emerged from the able and committed people who founded the first co-operatives and built up the organisation. This generation is now within ten years of retirement age, so that a relatively large number of senior positions will soon have to be filled. Most of the associated co-operatives are quite small businesses offering little opportunity for management development. Business education is not geared to instilling the attitudes needed to keep up the traditions of the co-operatives, and in any case people who did not grow up with these traditions might not be attracted by the relatively low managerial salaries offered within the Group. The response to the problem was to set up, in 1984, the Co-operative and Business Training Centre, IKASBIDE, linked to the general technical secretariat of the Caja Laboral. In January 1985, the first class of one hundred new graduates — without work experience — started on a two year course of theoretical and practical training. At the mid-way point the numbers had fallen quite sharply but those who complete the course will be offered jobs in the co-operatives at the end. Courses will also be run for working managers who will be able to attend courses to upgrade their professional skills in the parallel Management Development Programme. IKASBIDE will also provide library and information services. The first year's budget is 212 million pesetas.

The initiative springs from the realisation that the world has changed, that Mondragón is no longer the close-knit community where people set up or joined co-operatives as a matter of course, and that it now takes a mix of people with just the right combination of skills to start a viable business. Don José María Arizmendiarrieta wrote (freely translated): 'There can be no co-operation without co-operators' and 'People do not normally become co-operators spontaneously, they have to be taught — the soil may be fertile but it has to be cultivated'. The up and coming young people in the Group have no doubt that the soil is still fertile.

By 1985 the Mondragón Group had grown from small beginnings into a conglomerate employing around nineteen thousand people and its institutions had evolved into the structure that successfully weathered the recession years. But growth had made the the bank's position difficult and the organisation unwieldy. The time was ripe for change, and after a great deal of discussion a significantly different new structure was designed. This is described in the next chapter.

3 The new structure of the Mondragón Group

The inaugural session on 19 December 1984 of the Co-operative Congress and Council of Groups marked the beginning of a new era: the Mondragón Group had created a new superstructure and put the Caja Laboral Popular on the same level as all the other co-operatives. All large organisations change their structure from time to time, but this was a major break with tradition. Membership of the Group had always meant association with the Caja Laboral. Leadership was largely in the hands of the Caja Laboral's directors, and its management services department, the División Empresarial carried out most of the head office functions. In the new structure there will be a supervisory body, the Co-operative Congress, and a top management body, the Council of Groups. The head office functions continue to be performed by the División Empresarial, but this has become a separate entity answering to the Council of Groups. Figure 3.1 gives an outline of the new structure.

The Co-operative Congress is composed of 350 members elected by the individual co-operatives roughly in proportion to the number of worker-members; it will meet at least once every two years, and its resolutions will normally be of the nature of recommendations to the Council of Groups or to individual co-operatives; its main purpose is to lay down policy guide lines on matters such as the promotion of new co-operatives, social security, training, research and development and external relations.

Figure 3.1   The new structure of the Mondragón group

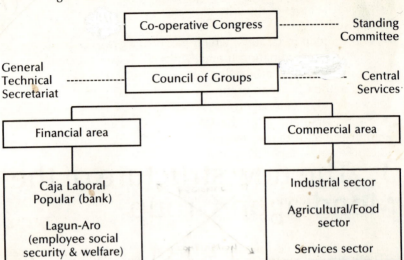

A standing committee of (at present) seventeen members of the Co-operative Congress, including its Chairman and Vice-Chairman, has the task of ensuring that decisions are implemented by co-operative groupings at every level, and ultimately by the individual co-operatives, which must pass appropriate resolutions in their own assemblies. The standing committee convenes the meetings of Congress and sets the agenda, which will always include the election of a new Chairman and Vice-Chairman.

To co-ordinate their policies and to share some administrative functions, the individual co-operatives are organised in a matrix of regional and sectoral groups. About seventy of the industrial co-operatives are at present associated in twelve regional groups — *Grupos Comarcales* — which formulate common social policies and working conditions, arrange transfers of members between them, and share some of the personnel, legal and financial administration. At the same time, the individual co-operatives belong to sectoral groups, whose purpose it is to co-ordinate the policies of co-operatives in the same line of business, to ensure that they do not compete with each other where this is not beneficial, and to help them jointly to achieve economies of scale. Groups have been organised on a regional basis since 1965, when ULARCO was formed in and around Mondragón itself, and most of them are now active. The three sectors of the commercial area in Figure 3.1 are still being organised.

The Council of Groups, which meets at least once a quarter, has the task of co-ordinating the activities of all the co-operatives, and when necessary of arbitrating between them. The Council is composed of the Chairman of the Co-operative Congress; the directors-general of the regional groups and of the retail co-operative EROSKI; the directors-general of the Caja Laboral, Lagun-Aro and IKERLAN; and the director of the División Empresarial. Council members have multiple votes depending on the size of the group they represent. Council decisions — which must of course be in accord with the policies laid down by Congress — have executive force.

The new structure preserves the principle that the group should function as a coherent whole with strong central management while preserving the spirit of voluntary association and self-management in the individual co-operatives. These remain separate legal entities voluntarily conferring powers on the central management, which they themselves control through the elected Congress.

The Caja Laboral has grown from a local savings bank into a large regional bank in Spain with 164 branches and resources amounting to 187,000 million pesetas. What signalled the need for change was that the proportion of these resources that could be invested in the co-operatives was shrinking fast (see Chapter 4). This did not make it impossible for the bank to manage the industrial co-operatives through one of its departments, but it meant that the management had to serve interests that were sometimes in conflict, and this was felt to be wrong.

The leading thinkers of the Group, many of whom have been with it from the beginning, are based in the Caja Laboral, and it was the Caja Laboral itself that started the process of change. The legitimacy of its dominant role was not in question — as a second-degree co-operative it was in a sense merely the other co-operatives' instrument. But as a general bank rather than purely as the co-operatives' house bank it has to assess investments inside and outside the Group by the same standards. It had become increasingly difficult to apply these standards objectively, and some of the leaders felt that the intimate relationship had made it dangerously easy for the co-operatives to raise money from the Caja Laboral. The new organisation would relieve the bank of its paternalistic role

HELP TOUGHER ATTITUDE TOWARDS cust.

23

towards the co-operatives and help it to adopt a tougher attitude towards them as creditors.

The Caja Laboral will of course continue to hold a special position among the co-operatives because — apart from some state investment grants — it is their sole source of funds for investment, working capital and personal loans to members. On average roughly half the co-operatives' capital is represented by loans from the Caja Laboral. So far, at least, there is no suggestion that the co-operatives should borrow from other sources, and it is difficult to imagine that other lenders would be more sympathetic to their needs. Seen from the bank's point of view, it still has more than a quarter of its funds tied up in the co-operatives, so it will give them the care and attention any bank must give to such a major creditor. The Caja Laboral is still very much a local bank, or at most a regional bank, with responsibilities to the community both as savers and as co-operators.

It remains to be seen how the new separate role of the División Empresarial will work out. Will its professional advice carry the same authority when it no longer represents the bank to whom those who need the advice are in debt? And will it be able to monitor the co-operatives' financial performance in the same way as a department of the bank, or will a new audit department be needed?

The new structure represents the best available compromise between hard realities and the aspirations of the co-operatives' rank-and-file members to own and control their enterprises. It is not derived from any dogma; like everything else at Mondragón it will be regarded as an experiment, and if necessary it will be changed.

4   Financial institutions: the Bank and Social Security

The Group's bank: Caja Laboral Popular

The Caja Laboral (in Basque — *Lan Kide Aurrezkia*) was set up in 1959 to provide financial services for its associated co-operatives and their members, and until very recently this remained its sole formal corporate objective; for more than a quarter of a century it was quite different from other co-operative banks and institutions like thrift and loan societies and credit unions; as a bank dedicated to meet the financial needs of a group of mainly industrial co-operatives it may indeed have been unique. The Group's growth in the late sixties and early seventies was for all practical purposes bank driven, and it is hard to imagine that the co-operatives would have been able to finance their development from other more conventional sources. Now, however, the bank's ability to attract funds has outstripped the investment opportunities offered by the co-operatives. By the early 1980s it ranked twenty-sixth among the top three hundred banking institutions in Spain. It has since obtained the national and regional authorities' approval to lend to conventional private businesses in the Basque region. The re-organisation of the co-operative Group will facilitate further expansion into more conventional banking activities.

The Spanish official gazette of July 1959 formally records the establishment of the first two branches of the Caja Laboral, one in Mondragón itself in the province of Guipúzcoa, and one in nearby Elorrio in the province of Vizcaya. The reason for starting two branches at once was the fear that the authorities in one or other of the provinces might be hostile to the initiative and would try to frustrate it. The idea, of course, had come from Arizmendiarrieta. He had worked out the legal basis and persuaded the leaders of ULGOR to take on the project and three other co-operatives — FUNCOR, ARRASATE and the first local consumer co-operative store — to join in. The legal form was that of a 'co-operative credit company', a category of savings bank that was allowed to pay 1% more interest than others in the heavily regulated Spanish system of that time.

More branches were set up quite soon in the heartland provinces Guipúzcoa and Vizcaya and a little later in the other Basque provinces. A Madrid branch was set up in 1980, but without any intention of changing the regional character of the bank. Tables 4.1 and 4.2 illustrate the history of growth: it was particularly rapid before the mid-1970s as might be expected, but it continued steadily through the recession, and has accelerated since to make the Caja Laboral one of the fastest-growing co-operatives in the group.

Table 4.1   Growth of the Caja Laboral Popular
Number of Branches

Year	Total	Guipúzcoa	Vizcaya	Alava	Navarra
1966	28	18	8	1	1
1973	63	35	18	5	5
1978	84	41	28	8	7
1983	141=	52	47	15	26
1984	153=	55	51	18	28
1985	164=	57	55	21	30

= including 1 in Madrid

Comparison with Table 2.1 shows that the bank's total resources amounted to less than a quarter of the group's turnover in 1965 and to just over half in 1970; they had almost drawn level by 1980 and they now exceed sales by one-third.

The bank has been profitable throughout its history. The gross surplus grew particularly fast between 1983 and 1984 when it increased by nearly a half. Though the surplus has since levelled off in real terms, the 1985 Annual Report still shows a gross figure of 3.3 thousand million pesetas — 2.7 thousand million net after interest and taxes. In 1985 the co-operatives' stake in the bank earned them, in addition to interest, a distribution amounting to one-third of their new investments in industrial activities.

Table 4.2   Growth of the Caja Laboral Popular

	Resources in pesetas of 1985 (thousand millions)			
Year	Deposits	Total resources A	Investment in co-operatives B	B as % of A
1960	—	0.1	—	52
1961	0.1	0.2	0.1	51
1962	0.3	0.5	0.3	66
1963	1.0	1.3	1.0	72
1964	1.6	2.2	1.7	77
1965	3.4	4.6	3.4	73
1966	5.7	6.5	4.7	72
1967	8.3	9.2	6.6	72
1968	11.2	13.0	9.2	71
1969	17.9	20.6	13.2	64
1970	23.1	26.9	15.8	59
1971	30.9	35.3	19.2	54
1972	38.8	44.4	22.1	50
1973	46.1	52.6	24.2	46
1974	53.8	61.6	31.5	51
1975	59.8	69.1	36.6	53
1976	66.7	77.2	38.6	50
1977	68.7	79.9	40.6	51
1978	74.6	86.8	41.5	48
1979	82.2	95.9	47.3	49
1980	88.9	105.3	45.9	44
1981	96.4	121.9	48.8	40
1982	104.7	129.1	51.8	40
1983	115.4	141.4	51.4	36
1984	128.8	159.8	46.4	29
1985	147.0	187.0	47.1	25

Source: Caja Laboral Popular

Several factors have contributed to the Caja Laboral's success. In the earliest days it had the built-in advantages of roots in a close-knit community. As a savings bank, even though it paid the best rate of interest, it was able to borrow cheaply. Most of its resources are deposits even today, and the 1985 balance sheet shows that about 15% of the total resources are in current accounts and another 27% are in savings accounts. It also enjoys a marginal cost advantage over other banks because of the compressed salary scales common to all the co-operatives in the Group, and presumably some advantage from its own employees' motivation and their awareness of the key role they play in the whole operation. Administrative costs too are relatively low since there is no need to attract private and institutional shareholders and to handle dividend payments.

The Caja Laboral's special position in and around Mondragón itself has been eroded by the liberalisation of banking and its own geographical spread, but it has meanwhile evolved an array of depositor-friendly marketing policies. Under Spanish law the depositors in a credit co-operative cannot at the same time be shareholders, but the Caja Laboral effectively treats them as such by holding depositors' general meetings. These meetings are attended by thousands of depositors who listen carefully to presentations of the latest results and announcements of plans and evidently feel that the bank has their interests at heart. Unquestionably there is also some general sympathy among the Basque public for a bank with an explicit policy to create and sustain employment in the region. But what savings bank depositors look for first and foremost is security, and the Caja Laboral has an admirable record of prudent investment, with considerably more than the statutory minimum in inter-bank deposits and officially approved securities, and most careful monitoring of the performance of the associated co-operatives as commercial borrowers. Since there are no private or institutional shareholders who might invest in the bank for income, a high proportion of the profits can be ploughed back into investment — until recently all investment within the Group, while the rest was mostly placed on the inter-bank market and in government stocks.

In the growth period of the 1970s the Caja Laboral was able to finance not only manufacturing plant but also much new building by the Group's housing co-operatives. Lending to co-operatives is normally on profitable commercial terms, but the Caja Laboral's first objective is to keep the co-operatives in being, and interest can be reduced or even waived in cases of hardship. In the early 1980s the bank stepped up its efforts to seek out opportunities for new ventures, and to help re-structure older co-operatives to meet the tougher competitive conditions. In many respects the bank was the main driving force behind the Group's development.

The Caja Laboral also provides a significant number of jobs. In the past decade its contribution of new jobs has been second only to that of the retail chain EROSKI. In 1975 the bank employed 587 people or 4.2% of the membership of the whole Group; by 1984 the number had more than doubled, to 1226 people or 6.4% of the membership.

Management services: División Empresarial

The Caja Laboral has always been more than a bank. It was set up by the founders of the industrial co-operative ULGOR at Arizmendiarrieta's instigation and no doubt already in 1959 as part of his concept of a much larger group of co-operatives. Since the same people were involved, the Caja Laboral was quite naturally the seat of the Group's central management. By 1969 the Group had grown to forty-six associated co-operatives with nearly 8000 members, and the managerial activities could evidently no longer be handled informally. A separate division was set up under the name of División Empresariál (in Basque — *Lan Kide Suztaketa*), which conveys its purpose rather better than our English translation: it exists not only to provide the co-operative enterprises with managerial help and advice in financial, legal and administrative matters, but also to stimulate and support entrepreneurial activity — to promote innovation and diversification in existing co-operatives, to do the preparatory work for setting up new co-operatives and to help to get them started, and generally to improve the Group's performance and promote its growth.

Under the new organisation these functions are no longer carried out within the bank but in a separate entity answerable to and represented on the Council of Groups. The ultimate intention is to make this entity into a self-financing co-operative, but for the time being it has the legal form of a wholly-owned subsidiary company of the Caja Laboral (División Empresariál SA, *Lan Kide Suztaketa SA* or simply LKS) and the staff remain members of the Caja Laboral. At present LKS does not charge the Caja Laboral for its services, and it is required to recover only 60% of its costs from within the Group; but it will be able to derive additional income by selling consultancy services to clients outside the Group, and the ultimate intention is to make it into a self-financing co-operative. To judge by the publicity brochure, an effort is clearly being made to project a commercial image, and the more independent role is underlined by the recent move to a separate new building. There is also some decentralisation by secondment of specialist staff to the headquarters of regional subgroups.

This process of evolution is a neat demonstration of the Group's adaptability. LKS has a staff of over well over one hundred, organised in seven 'areas', some of them subdivided into departments:-
- Market research and evaluation — research, library
- Agriculture and food business promotion
- Industrial business promotion
- Audit and financial records & forecasts
- Managerial control and assistance (*Intervención*)
- Consultancy (*Asesoriamiento*) — marketing, production engineering, personnel, organisation, law and tax
- Building — planning, industrial, housing

The functions of the various consultancy departments and those of the building departments are adequately described by their titles, but the business promotion and *intervención* areas bear a characteristic Mondragón stamp and need explanation.

The contract of association provides that the Caja Laboral should carry out an audit of the associated co-operatives' accounts once every four years. This alone would merely be in the interests of economy and convenience, but supervision does not stop there. The co-operatives submit an annual management plan and a five-year long-term plan; their sales records and order books are open to inspection, as are their staff records; and they provide a monthly financial report. All this information — more than some conglomerate companies would collect from their subsidiaries — is collated by the financial records department for purposes of overall Group planning. Routine collection of information also serves to give early warning of potential problems in the individual co-operatives, in which case the managerial controllers may come in. In Spanish, an *interventor* is strictly speaking a comptroller or auditor, whose role is to check and certify the accounts and who would normally intervene only when a company was practically on the rocks. But at Mondragón the *intervención* department can and does intervene before the trouble gets too serious and tries to effect a turn-round. A co-operative may have to accept an *interventor* on its board as a 'company doctor', change its management, and follow an imposed recovery plan; the Caja Laboral helps to sort out the financial side, but if and when the co-operative comes back into profit it gets a 5% share for the next two years. The changes imposed can be quite radical — there have been cases where a co-operative has switched to a completely different product within a year. Some fifteen co-operatives might be on the 'sick list' at any one time.

The Mondragón Group justly prides itself in its sustained effort to find new business opportunities, the deliberate effort to enlarge its membership in the growth phase, and the present effort to keep up with new technology. It also used to make it a rule that new co-operatives had to be generated from the bottom up: whether or not it had been its idea in the first place, the División Empresariál required that a small number of founder members of the new co-operative appeared before it as promoters, whose plans were then subjected to a most searching and often prolonged examination before they were accepted into association with the Caja Laboral. It was relatively easy to stick to this rule while much of the growth was in medium-technology engineering products for the home market, and prospective members of the new co-operative such as skilled engineering workers could readily understand the market as well as the production technology. Now that the technology has become much more specialised and the markets more international it is hardly possible to make plans for a new business without expert help. Recently, therefore, the División Empresariál has relaxed the 'bottom-up' rule and its pre-feasibility studies may make off-the-shelf plans — complete with financing arrangements incorporating government subsidies — available to groups of workers who wish to start a new co-operative. The creation of the co-operative IKUS to make spectacle frames — quite a new product for the Group — is a favourite example. The general policy is nevertheless quite the contrary of indiscriminate diversification: the promotion departments are primarily looking for natural extensions of existing business; but in these days of rapid technological change it is often not obvious what could sensibly be grafted on, the net must be cast wide, and much imagination is needed to spot the real opportunities.

If one factor can be singled out as responsible for the success of the Mondragón co-operatives it is that even the smallest of them is both assisted and disciplined by a battery of management services on a scale appropriate to a company as big as the whole Group.

The Group's Social Security organisation: Lagun-Aro

In Spain members of workers' co-operatives are classed as self-employed, for whom health, pensions and unemployment insurance are normally provided by the authorised mutual fund for the self-employed, *Mutualidad de Trabajadores Autónomos*. When the first Mondragón co-operatives were started it was natural that the Caja Laboral should act as broker. In October 1959, within months of being formally registered as a bank, the Caja Laboral began to provide a social security service.

The *Mutualidad Autónomos* did not meet the needs of the Mondragón co-operatives: it was expensive for a young and healthy population — the median age is in the mid-thirties even today — and it was designed for individual businesses and could not provide a mechanism for mutual help. At the end of 1966 the Group was given official approval to insure the membership — at that time 5,100 — collectively in a separate complementary scheme, then already called 'Lagun-Aro'. Meanwhile an altogether new scheme was being worked out, and in June 1969 'Lagun-Aro, Mutua' was registered as a separate insurance fund which was affiliated to the *Mutualidad Autónomos* but operated under its own rules.

At the end of 1973 the Caja Laboral set up Lagun-Aro as a new second degree co-operative, a hybrid governed by both co-operative and mutual insurance legislation. Because of legal complexities Lagun-Aro did not become an associated co-operative of the Caja Laboral until 1977. Finally, in 1984, the Lagun-Aro statutes were revised for registration under the law of the Basque autonomous region.

In the last few years Spanish social security legislation has been reformed and further changes are under discussion. Lagun-Aro has been in negotiation with the authorities about the extent to which it must now be integrated with the state-authorised fund. So far only the pensions scheme has been affected: since 1984 part of the contribution collected by Lagun-Aro has been paid over to the *Mutualidad Autónomos*, and the total contribution has gone up from 18.5% to 20.25% of earnings without adding anything to the pension rights. Members are however still much better off: the state pension, after thirty years' contributions, is only 40% of final earnings, and in the pure state scheme they would have to contribute 28.8% of earnings; under the combined scheme, the Lagun-Aro fund makes up the pension to the previous level of 60%.

The state will no doubt make further inroads into the Lagun-Aro system eventually, but the co-operatives' leadership will be in no hurry to move in that direction. The separate scheme not only provides cheaper insurance, both because of the composition of the membership and because administration costs are lower for a captive clientele, but also because Lagun-Aro makes an important contribution to the spirit of co-operation across the Group. In one way or another the three basic principles of the system all reflect the Group's philosophy.

The first principle is that contributions and benefits are partly fixed and partly earnings-related. All members are treated as equals as regards their families' needs, medical expenses and death benefits, and these are therefore covered by the flat-rate contribution, as is the cost of administration. But equality does not extend to retirement, widows' and disability pensions, nor to unemployment benefit — for these both contributions and benefits are earnings-related. And since solidarity between members of different earning capacity is expressed in the narrow range between top and bottom earnings, there is no element of redistribution between them in the social security system: the variable part of contributions and benefits is simply proportional to earnings.

The second principle is that only the pensions are financed through an invested fund and all other benefits are paid out of current contributions. The pension fund is invested in approved securities, in part directly and in part through the *Mutualidad Autónomos*, to protect it from the co-operatives' business risks to which the rest of the members' assets are exposed. Moreover, to make up to some extent for the erosion of pensions by inflation, the fund is topped up out of the pay-as-you-go part of the contribution. Many companies top up their pension funds out of profits, but as usual the Mondragón way is different and designed to remind members that the money used is their own. So far very little has had to be spent in this way since there are only about four hundred pensioners. An increase in the number of pensioners is foreseeable, but the projections give no cause for alarm.

Contributions other than those made under the heading of pensions amount to about 40% of the total. It is recalculated annually from the benefits paid out the year before, making it very clear where the money goes: about 14% on medical expenses, another 12% on sickness benefit, and about 6% on family allowances. Unemployment benefit took up only 1.6% of the contribution in 1982-84; in 1985 this nearly tripled to 4.6% but remained well below the premium of the *Mutualidad Autónomos* which would have been 6.4%.

The total Lagun-Aro contribution amounts to about 32% of average earnings, but the flat-rate element makes it somewhat regressive so that it rises to about 36% at the bottom end of the wage scale. At first sight the contribution seems inordinately high, though with income tax at around only 15% the average wage earners' total deductions are not very different in Spain from those in other countries. However, members of co-operatives pay more because they are self-employed and therefore pay what would be the employer's social security contribution.

The third principle is 'inter-co-operative solidarity', which means that co-operatives or the subgroups called 'communities' (largely the same as the regional subgroups of the business organisation) must to some extent subsidise each other's medical expenses and sickness benefit, and that some benefits are designed to protect the co-operatives as much as the individual. In other words, the social security system is not purely an insurance scheme but may be used as an instrument of Group policy.

For many years the main application of the solidarity principle was the system of community surcharges and bonuses for overspending and underspending on medical expenses and sickness benefit. Lagun-Aro keeps very detailed sickness and accident statistics and from them calculates annual budgets for the communities. If a community overspends its budget by more than 10% it is surcharged, and if it underspends gets back half the saving. This combination of a no claim bonus from the insurance scheme with the equivalent of a large company's inter-plant competition was very effective in the days of growth and full employment: absenteeism was held to approximately half the average level in other firms*.

It was during the recession of the early 1980s and in its aftermath, however, that Lagun-Aro proved to be a particularly powerful and valuable instrument of Group policy. The basic aim was to keep every member of a co-operative employed within the Group. When it became essential to the survival of many co-operatives to make big reductions in manning, Lagun-Aro gave some incentives to encourage early retirement but made it almost impossible to make people redundant. Instead, it provided all kinds of help for people who could not be relocated within their regional subgroup.

For transfers to a co-operative in a different subgroup Lagun-Aro provides quite handsome relocation benefits such as travel expenses in the case of temporary transfers, cheap loans to help with rehousing if the transfer is permanent, and contributions towards the maintenance of earnings if the transfer is to a lower-grade job. For people whose old co-operative has lost some or all of their capital Lagun-Aro makes up what they need for the capital stake in their new co-operative — often the most important benefit. But the conditions that have to be met to qualify for these benefits are very stiff: the co-operative that wishes to transfer people out has to prove that it needs to cut back by at least forty people or a fifth of its workforce; it must stop distributing profits, if any, to its members and paying out the interest on their individual shareholdings; and it must cut its members' wages to bring them down, grade for grade, to 85% of those on the Caja Laboral's scale. Table 4.3 below shows the number of transfers assisted in some way by Lagun-Aro.

These policies have naturally aroused a good deal of debate in the Group. One issue has been that the belt-tightening falls unevenly on different regional subgroups, especially since those that can transfer members of ailing co-operatives within the subgroup get no help from Lagun-Aro. Another issue was that the co-operatives cannot take full advantage of the state assistance available for restructuring

* From a study by the San Sebastián Chamber of Commerce in 'Mondragón: an economic analysis' by Henk Thomas and Chris Logan, George Allen & Unwin, 1982.

Table 4.3   Assisted transfers between co-operatives

Year	Permanent	Temporary	Total
1982	109	314	423
1983	62	428	490
1984	99	322	421
1985	109	416	525

certain industry sectors (such as machine tools) if they refuse to let people go and accept redundancy payments; the alternative of accepting funds for re-equipment is not always a realistic option. The wisdom of staying out of the state unemployment insurance scheme is also being questioned; Lagun-Aro contributions will of course be lower as long as the policy of not allowing members to become unemployed can be so rigidly maintained, but some members feel that the sacrifices needed to avoid redundancies are stretching solidarity a bit too far.

However, the Group has in fact survived the recession with only a handful of outright redundancies in a region that was among the worst hit in Spain. With less rigorous policies the co-operatives' commitment to keeping all their members on board in a storm might have been weakened, and so might the resolve to create new jobs now that better times may be in sight. The regional subgroups, to which so much importance is attached in the new Group organisation, may now have a breathing space to build up their reserves and their job-creation effort — in fact to replicate locally a combination of Lagun-Aro and the División Empresariál. The next storm in the form of competition from other EEC countries may not be far away.

Lagun-Aro made its own contribution to job creation by branching out into household and motor insurance. Seguros Lagun-Aro SA was split off in 1982 and now employs about 20 people (Lagun-Aro itself employs about 40). With the advantages of low overheads and a natural clientele it came into profit almost immediately, so it will be possible, eventually, to reconstitute it as a new co-operative.

5 Industrial co-operatives and local groups

The co-operatives associated with the Mondragón Group at the beginning of 1986 are listed in Appendix B. Only a few can be individually described in this book, and such a small sample cannot be fully representative of so many co-operatives of different sizes in different kinds of business. But to appreciate that they really are individual co-operatives owned by their members rather than branches or wholly-owned subsidiaries of a conglomerate company it is necessary to shift the focus away from the centre. The old structure in which the Group's headquarters were to all intents and purposes identified with the Caja Laboral obscured its function as a service to the associated co-operatives. In the new structure the bank is shown as a business in its own right alongside the associated co-operatives, over them all is the Council of Groups, and an important formal role is thus assigned to the regional and sectoral subgroups. Some of these subgroups as yet exist only on paper, but enough of them have been in operation for long enough to show how the two-tier structure works in practice. The main purpose of the thumbnail sketches in this chapter, however, is to describe a varied selection of rank-and-file co-operatives to illustrate some of the struggles and achievements of a cross-section of the Group's 19,000 worker-owners.

The Mondragón regional group ULARCO

The first local subgroup with some shared functions was set up by ULGOR and three other co-operatives in 1964, by which time the Group as a whole had grown to twenty-nine co-operatives and extended beyond the immediate vicinity of Mondragón. ULGOR had started by making oil-fired cooking stoves, and when bottled butane became available soon afterwards it switched to making gas cookers under licence from an Italian firm. Sales of these cookers grew very fast, and in 1963 ULGOR also branched out into making refrigerators. Both were marketed under the brand name FAGOR which has now — since January 1986 — been adopted for all of ULARCO's products.

New opportunities were thus created for component suppliers, and there were obvious advantages in a degree of vertical integration. ARRASATE, an old co-operative making stampings and lawn mowers, was persuaded to switch to making heavy machine tools of the kind needed to produce parts for domestic appliances. A new co-operative COPRECI was set up to manufacture components. Two small private iron foundries in nearby Eskoriatza were converted into one co-operative under the name of EDERLAN. Between 1960 and 1964 these co-operatives increased their combined sales sixfold in real terms; their membership then grew explosively and continued to grow quite rapidly until well into the 1970s.

Table 5.1   Membership of the ULARCO co-operatives

Year	1960	1962	1963	1964	1969	1974	1979	1985
ULGOR	228	429	600	816	2030	3284	3855	2256
others	37	69	304	534	2008	2616	2825	4126
Total	265	498	904	1350	4038	5900	6680	6382

Sources: Thomas & Logan (see Chapter 4)
Caja Laboral (1985 figures)

By the end of the 1970s the number of co-operatives in the group had grown to eight: the production of electronic components had been transferred out of ULGOR to make the separate co-operative FAGOR ELECTROTECNICA in 1966 and the production of industrial catering and laundry equipment as FAGOR INDUSTRIAL in 1973; a new co-operative, RADAR, had established itself in Eskoriatza to make kitchenware such as pressure cookers; the student co-operative ALECOOP (see Chapter 6) also makes components for household appliances.

Not included in the total above are the 275 members of a co-operative which is also located at Mondragón but not engaged in manufacturing: AUZO LAGUN, whose main business is industrial contract catering and cleaning.

The ULARCO subgroup continued to create new co-operatives in the early 1980s and so helped to maintain employment during the recession. As a rule, existing co-operatives would diversify into new products and then set up the departments that made them as new co-operatives. Thus ULGOR, which had to slim down its core work-force quite drastically, reconstituted the domestic electrical equipment side under the name of FAGOR; and the production of domestic water and space heating equipment became FAGOR CLIMA. At about the same time the new co-operative ORKLI was formed as a spin-off from COPRECI to make control valves for gas appliances. Other new co-operatives were set up in related lines of business: AURKI to produce numerical control and other automation devices, LEUNKOR to take on light machining work for short runs of special-ised parts, and LENNIZ to manufacture kitchen furniture. Thus although it counts as one of the regional subgroups, ULARCO is quite a well-integrated business in the general area of mainly electrical home and kitchen equipment, domestic 'white goods' and their industrial counterparts.

ULGOR itself has always been the odd man out among the Mondra-gon co-operatives because of the sheer size of its workforce which reached a peak of 3,855 in 1979. In 1974 it had a full-blooded industrial strike — as distinct from the fairly frequent stoppages to express solidarity with Basque political demands in the later years of the Franco era — which has not happened before or since in any of the Group's other co-operatives. Only a minority of the workforce - about four hundred people — came out, and the strike lasted just eight days. But the incident was regarded as serious enough for ULGOR's general assembly to endorse the management's recom-mendation to expel the seventeen ringleaders and to impose penalties on all the other strikers. Ostensibly the strike was about a job-regrading exercise, but in reality it was probably a symptom of a breakdown of communications in an organisation that had grown too fast. In fact, the people who had been thrown out in 1974 were amnestied ten years later, but it seems that not many wanted to come back.

By the end of 1985 the workforce had come down to about 2,200 — still two and a half times as many as in the next largest co-operative — and by 1990 it may have to shrink by another two or three hundred. Most of the slimming has been achieved by diversification as described, but the workforce was brought down by another 466 by persuading the after-sales service people to exchange their membership of the co-operative for contracts as self-employed operators, with an option to re-join within a stipulated period if this did not work out. Despite these reductions, the workforce that remained had to tighten its belt quite considerably, awarding themselves pay increases that did not keep pace with the cost of living and forgoing, in some years, the customary payment of a thirteenth and fourteenth month's salary: by 1983 ULGOR came back into profit.

A major programme of restructuring the product range is now in progress: dishwashers are a fairly recent addition; the range of refrigerators has already been redesigned; new lines in gas and electric cookers are due to be in production by the end of 1987 while other heating appliances have been dropped; and a two-year restructuring programme for washing machines is due to start at the end of 1986. There will be capacity for the annual production of 150,000 dishwashers, 400,000 refrigerators, 500,000 cookers and ovens and 350,000 washing machines. Productivity will be substantially improved, especially in the cooker and ovens plant, which is being redesigned in collaboration with Hitachi.

In 1983 the business magazine 'Dinero' named ULGOR as one of Spain's ten most exemplary enterprises — six of which were subsidiaries of multinationals. In the Spanish government's proposed restructuring of the domestic appliance industry into three groups, one is based on ULGOR and the other two on the multinationals Philips and Electrolux. Despite these achievements, of which it is understandably proud, ULGOR faces formidable competition in a business where there is gross overcapacity throughout Europe. ULGOR expects to maintain an exclusive position in some lines tailored to special market needs, but it is no secret that its white goods sales overall declined sharply in 1983-84 and recovered only partially in 1985. Herculean efforts will be needed to attract and retain customer loyalty in Spain and elsewhere in Europe — an important first step is the recent decision to promote the brand image of all the ULARCO products under the single brand name FAGOR.

The DEBAKO machine tool group

Four of the ten co-operatives in the machine tool business are associated in the group DEBAKO. They have about 850 members between them and in 1984 their turnover was 3.6 million pesetas. This group has its headquarters in a modern industrial estate outside the old industrial town of Elgoibar, about 15 miles from Mondragón. Two of the co-operatives in the group are not in Elgoibar, but they are within about ten miles, so the group is geographically compact and in fact counts as one of the regional groups. But the main purpose of the grouping is joint investment planning and product development, and joint marketing in the more distant and the smaller markets where it would be uneconomic to maintain separate agencies. Some economic and financial services are also shared, but separate accounts are kept for each of the four co-operatives.

DANOBAT, the largest of the four co-operatives, predates the Mondragón Group: it was founded in 1952 and did not join the Group until 1963; it now has about 560 members, not far below its peak. The main product lines have always been grinding machines and lathes, which now appear in their modern guise as numerically controlled machines; later, automatic handling equipment was added to the range, and, quite recently, robots. The managers are very much aware of the competitive pressures: they expect more competition in the home market as a result of Spain's entry into the EEC, and they are somewhat concerned that exports have recently fallen from their peak of 50% to below 40% of the output. They realise that their future depends on remaining internationally competititive, they are putting much effort into the development — partly in collaboration with the Group's central research unit IKERLAN — of new products, including control equipment and software. They maintain their own sales agency, Danobat Inc, in Chicago, and agencies in Britain, France and Germany, and they have a subsidiary co-operative with 18 members in Mexico.

GOITI, the other co-operative in Elgoibar itself, is much smaller. It has about eighty members, whose main activity is the manufacture of presses; but for historical reasons they also undertake some quite unrelated contract work. GOITI was formed in 1962 and associated with the Group in 1965. Even then it was advised by the Caja Laboral Popular to give up the contracting business, and having recently been drastically restructured with the CLP's help, it is about to do this. In collaboration with a Japanese partner, they intend to make GOITI the national leader (and eventually an effective competitor within the European Community) in the manufacture of numerically controlled punching presses. This may be a problem as half the work-force is over fifty.

SORALUCE, was formed in 1962 to manufacture drilling machines, which remains the main activity. The forty-two founder-members, associated with the Mondragón group from the beginning, invested the then very considerable sum of 4 million pesetas. The membership rose to a peak of 214 and has since fallen back to below 190. Like all machine tools, drilling machines have been technically transformed in the last ten years, by numerical control and by incorporation in multi-purpose machining centres, so that the mechanical part now represents barely 50% of the value, and electronics between 30 and 40%. SORALUCE is about to embark on a major research and development effort in collaboration with the cooperative AURKI which makes numerical controls and with the central research unit IKERLAN. 60% of the output is exported, so technical development is clearly important; and for such a small co-operative, association with the DEBAKO group provides very useful economies of scale.

TXURTXIL, in Bergara, had been, under another name, an ordinary limited company making grinding machines. When this failed, 62 of its 88 employees decided to form a co-operative under the auspices of the Mondragón Group, with which it became formally associated in 1979. Under the business plan worked out with the Caja Laboral, the new co-operative would design and make a grinding machine complementary to DANOBAT's product range; this has been selling well. In 1980 it was decided to branch out into spark erosion machines in partnership with a British firm which supplies the electrical equipment. This is the reason for the English name — Txurtxil is the Basque spelling of Churchill. The managers believe that they will be able to hold their own with their conventional machines for two or three more years, until they have developed an electronics-based product range for the future; they are confident that they can restructure the membership to bring in enough people with electronics skills.

The DEBAKO group is controlled by a board consisting of two directors-general of its own and ten directors of the constituent co-operatives. The group's rules require that decisions should be reached by consensus. But subject to this consensus the contractual relationship of the constituent co-operatives to the group is felt to be binding, though it has no legal status and seems to be less formal than the association with the main Mondragón Group. DEBAKO is managed by its two directors-general and five managers, located in modest offices in the DANOBAT building.

One of the obligations of group membership is that profitable co-operatives must pay over part of their profits to others that make losses. The amount is determined by a formula: 25% of a co-operative's profits go to its own reserves, and before the rest is distributed to the members' accounts, up to 50% is put into the group's loss compensation pool; if this is not enough, the rest of the loss is presumably borne by the loss-making co-operative's members. When a co-operative falls upon hard times so that it can no longer find work for all its members, it is in the first instance up to the group to arrange re-deployment internally and at its own expense. It is a bone of contention that the central funds of Lagun-Aro are available only when people transfer to co-operatives in another group (see Chapter 6), that there are not enough opportunities for such transfers to allow the group to cut back its workforce in line with the structural changes in the machine tool industry, and that Lagun-Aro has not, at least until recently, made provision for redundancies and early retirement on a significant scale.

The machine tool industry has changed so dramatically that it is not surprising that people have lost faith in the possibility of solving the employment problem by transfers. In 1980, 95% of the product was still made in the manufacturer's mechanical engineering work-shops, but by 1984 bought-in control equipment accounted for about 40% of the value, while the mechanical parts had been simplified and required less labour. The DEBAKO co-operatives have developed their technology as fast as the ordinary limited com-panies, and they, too, get investment grants under the Basque

Regional Government's restructuring programme for the industry. But they cannot cut back the workforce in the same way and let the state look after the people who are no longer needed. The DEBAKO group's members are not primarily people with the right skills for the new technology — the Mondragón co-operative which does make numerical control equipment is not in the group — and the reduction in numbers by twenty-four between 1983 and 1984 was not enough to solve the manpower problem. Short-time working amounting to a 12% reduction in hours has had to be introduced throughout the group, with a corresponding reduction in take-home pay — maintenance of earnings would have been nonsensical since the money could only come out of the members' own pockets. But while the price of co-operative solidarity has been quite high, it is a matter of pride that a hundred or more redundancies have been avoided.

The Bilbao regional group NERBION

Greater Bilbao is not the most fertile ground for co-operatives. The city expanded rapidly with industrial growth in the sixties and early seventies, there is much widely dispersed new housing, and a large part of the population has no local roots. In the old industrial districts the tone is set by traditionally strong trade unions with little sympathy for the co-operative idea. In relation to the size of the working population the membership of Mondragón Group in the region is small — a little over five hundred; there are only seven co-operatives, mostly small, and some with an uncertain future. The group's total sales income is about 3500 million pesetas. But the NERBION regional management, headed by a former senior member of the División Empresarial, is set on restructuring the group to give it some coherence, and on promoting new co-operatives in high technology areas and not necessarily in manufacturing industry; they have already formed a co-operative of consulting engineer.

MATRICI, with over three hundred members and a sales income of about 1800 million pesetas, is by far the largest co-operative in the group. It is in the business of making moulds and dies, primarily the dies used in pressing steel sheets into motor car body sections; when a new model is brought out, the car manufacturers distribute their orders for dies — just one for each bit of body — among the small number of highly specialised firms around the world. MATRICI started in 1963 with twenty-nine members, and it is still expanding; it is among the world's leaders in the development of the technology, and it already has the full computer-aided design and manufacturing capability, though most car makers do not yet supply the design in numerical form. Its customers already include General Motors, Mercedes and Volvo, and it is currently attempting to enter both the British and the Japanese market.

MATRIPLAST was started in 1984 with forty-four members as a spin-off from MATRICI. Using simpler technology of the same kind, it makes moulds for motor car components made of plastics. Since the customers are the same, the products are marketed jointly with MATRICI. MATRIPLAST has its own board, but its profits are pooled with MATRICI.

ONA-PRES has been a manufacturer of heavy hydraulic presses for twenty-five years, but it was a limited company until about ten years ago and only joined the Mondragón Group in 1978; it now has eighty-five members and a sales of nearly 500 million pesetas. Though most of the sales are in the home market, the management believes that the technology is fully competitive. They are, however, worried about their cramped factory site in an old industrial part of the town — they have no room for expansion and they find it difficult to maintain the co-operative culture in an area where there is much labour discontent.

ELKAR is a co-operative with thirty-seven members in the printing business. It has been producing books, catalogues, calendars and the like since 1967, and seems to be on a steady course and able to take the technological changes in the industry in its stride.

BIHAR is a small electronics firm making specialised items of instrumentation and control, and providing a design and consultancy service. It was formed in 1981 by a group of eleven engineers from a private company that failed; it now has sixteen members and a turnover of 150 million pesetas.

ONDOAN is a firm of consulting engineers which started with four members in 1982, grew to over twenty in two years and is likely to go on growing. In 1984 the turnover reached about 240 million pesetas. ONDOAN designed the heating and air-conditioning in the new División Empresarial building at Mondragón, and boilers and other services for the new MATRIPLAST factory; but these are the only projects they have so far undertaken for other co-operatives. There is clearly scope for expansion in this direction.

CITAMARE, a traditional furniture manufacturing co-operative founded in 1966, which once employed ninety people, is in the process of being wound up. When the regional group was formed in 1980, a desperate attempt was made to restructure and modernise the business, and it was hoped to stabilise the workforce at thirty; but by 1984 it was down to a core of fifteen, and will disappear when the remaining stocks have been sold. The failure of a co-operative throws into sharp relief the extent to which its members are committed to it: the CITAMARE members not only lost their capital stake, they actually ended up in debt, remaining individually liable for part of the money they had collectively borrowed from the Caja Laboral. Fortunately it was possible for some of them to join MATRIPLAST; and since the normal take-home pay in MATRIPLAST is higher than it was in CITAMARE, they are able to save to build up their capital stake in their new co-operative. But since they are being relocated within their regional group, they get nothing from Lagun-Aro.

The rescue of the CITAMARE members was of course just the sort of contingency for which the regional group was conceived. The directors of NERBION accept this, and they have set up their fund for the purpose; they pool 25% of each co-operative's profit, distribute 5% and put the rest in the fund. They also aim to achieve some synergy within the group by making the co-operatives' marketing objectives converge. They believe that it will be increasingly difficult to set up new manufacturing co-operatives, but that co-operatives offer new opportunities for professional workers; and they see a possible future for the Bilbao-based group in the provision of a full range of technical services.

The retail stores chain EROSKI

In the 1960s traditional consumer co-operative societies were in decline in the Basque country as elsewhere because they could not keep pace with modernisation. Without economies of scale and supermarket outlets, the societies could not offer lower prices and better quality than their conventional competitors. Until recently, moreover, Spanish consumer co-operatives suffered from the additional disadvantage that they were allowed to sell only to their members. In 1969 a break-away group of enterprising people who had seen the writing on the wall and had studied developments in other countries decided to set up a retail co-operative on a new model; there was quite widespread interest in this at first, but ultimately only nine of the seventy-seven surviving societies — there had once been 162 — merged to set up what became EROSKI.

Ideologically, the new model is a beautiful compromise. To succeed under the present competitive conditions, the enterprise had to be large and centrally controlled. Where they had been so reorganised in other European countries, the co-operative idea was not much in evidence, and in the heartland of worker co-operatives it seemed incongruous that the workers had not been given a voice. Here, then, the natural solution was to make the new enterprise a workers' co-operative. But it would have been too much of a break with tradition simply to abandon the consumer interest, so there are also consumer members, and for them there are centrally organised activities and events. To ensure a proper balance between the two interests, the board of directors consists of six members elected by the employees and six elected by the consumers, and the chairman is always from the consumer side. An annual conference of employees and four geographically dispersed consumer conferences elect 250 delegates from each side to the general assembly which in turn elects the board.

The EROSKI management points with pride to the growing participation in consumer education activities in the last few years: in 1982 there were 172 events in which some seven thousand people took part; in 1984 there were over five hundred factory and headquarters visits, lectures and courses with over 80,000 participants, including five thousand children. There is also a stream of printed consumer information — in the weekly company paper, in its monthly supplement of special reports, and in consumer information sheets.

For its traditional clientele the co-op was a community meeting place, and consumerist activities are no substitute. But the future of large modern retail chains lies with large, high turnover, self-service stores, and it is difficult to run small neighbourhood stores within the same organisation. This problem has been solved by franchising private shopkeepers as exclusive outlets for goods supplied and priced by EROSKI, including of course house-branded goods. There were about 150 franchised shops in 1985, and also two cash-and-carry outlets. EROSKI has also recently acquired a travel agent's business with branches in Bilbao, Vitoria, San Sebastián and Pamplona. But the mainstream of the business consists of directly controlled branches — a chain of supermarkets, and, so far, one out-of-town hypermarket and one furniture store.

The growth of the business is illustrated by the following table:

Table 5.2   Evolution of the EROSKI retail chain 1979-84

Year	79	80	81	82	83	84
Sales						
in 1000 million pesetas	7.7	10.7	14.9	19.2	22.9	26.3
Number of stores	76	99	129	170	212	225
Worker-members	744	858	1008	1032	1078	1228
Consumer-members						
in thousands	102	104	105	110	123	131
Customer visits						
in millions	7.7	8.6	10.2	11.1	11.6	13.0

Source: *Trabajo y Unión*

EROSKI is one of the few fast-growing co-operatives in the Mondragón Group; the number of worker-members is expected to increase by about seven hundred in the next five years.

6 Education and Research

The early history of the Mondragón co-operative movement is so bound up with Arizmendiarrieta that his educational initiatives — the technical school set up in 1943 and the League of Education and Culture founded in 1948 — are regarded as the origins of the industrial co-operatives. Educational institutions have certainly always been an integral part of the movement, and they reflect his pragmatic philosophy: what was taught had above all to be capable of being put into practice, one could not get it right at the outset and should aim at progressive improvement rather than perfection — but one should be guided by a Utopian vision. And the vision, appropriate to the time, was roughly that if it provided itself with good technical education and training facilities the community would be able to pull itself up by its bootstraps.

Times have changed, but essentially the same tradition runs through the evolution of the technical school into a college of further and higher education, to the formation of the student-workers' co-operative ALECOOP in 1966, the creation of the Group research and development centre IKERLAN in 1977, and to the establishment of the management training centre IKASBIDE in 1984. Somewhat peripheral are the many non-vocational schools, most of which sprang up soon after Franco's death, when Basque-medium instruction was made legal but was not yet provided by the state; their association with the Mondragón Group is mainly a declaration of solidarity, since as parent-teacher co-operatives they are not really very similar. In the 1985 there were more than forty of these independent schools, nearly all of them in the provinces of Guipúzcoa and Vizcaya, but now they are gradually being absorbed into the state system.

Escuela Politecnica

The original technical school at Mondragón was supported by the community; it did not get a state subsidy until the 1950s, and it was officially recognised as a centre of technical education only in 1968. Finally, in 1976, it was designated a 'polytechnic institute' and could offer courses in university level technical engineering; but it continues to provide technical education at lower levels spanning the range between further and higher education (*Fachschule* and *Fachhochschule* in Germany). The total number of students reached a peak of about 1300 in 1976/77 and has declined to about 1200 since then. The course content has kept in step with the needs of the local industries: it now includes electronics and computer science as well as the more traditional metal work and mechanical and heavy electrical engineering.

The college is a special kind of second degree co-operative with three membership constituencies: teachers, students and parents, and supporting institutions. The supporting institutions are mainly the local industrial co-operatives; they cover the greater part of the running costs, while student fees and government grants may amount to no more than 20%. But the co-operatives' contributions, which come from their social funds, are a service to the community: the students need have no family connection with the co-operatives.

The worker-student co-operative ALECOOP

Students who have completed the two-year basic course at the technical college may earn their keep by joining the co-operative ALECOOP — the name is derived from *Actividad Laboral Escolar* — to work, with some teacher supervision, on a half-time basis compatible with college requirements. When the college started to organise student work in 1966 the experiment was viewed with suspicion and the industrial co-operatives offered only unskilled work. Nevertheless, ALECOOP was set up as an independent co-operative in 1970; it managed to win contracts for cable assemblies and mechanical and electrical components requiring at least semi-skilled work, and a few years later it began to develop products of its own. The most successful product so far is an electronics teaching kit for schools. ALECOOP now has its own factory but it will also send workers out to a customer's factory. The number of student-workers reached five hundred in 1980 and went down only marginally in the recession.

Like the college, ALECOOP has three membership constituencies: teacher-managers, worker-students, and industrial co-operatives as customers. But ALECOOP is self-financing — the customers pay on a cost basis at 90% of their own members' hourly rates. Like all members of a co-operative, the students have to make a capital contribution — in their case two months' wages saved up through deductions from wages. They have to pay college fees and, if they come from out of town, for board and lodging, so they are left with very little pocket money; but there is no shortage of applicants for membership.

The research and development centre IKERLAN

The individual industrial co-operatives are in general too small to develop enough radically new products themselves, and so they have always relied quite heavily on licensing. But to have an adequate understanding of the newest technologies, especially those based on micro-electronics, it is practically essential to do some in-house research. Some research is of course done by individual co-operatives, notably the machine tool and die makers who are developing numerical control systems and computer-aided design; but they too can benefit from having a centre of excellence within the Group, and some of them would not be able to keep up with the competition without it. Set up in 1977 to guard against this threat, IKERLAN now has a staff of about a hundred.

IKERLAN was instigated by the *Escuela Politecnica* and the Caja Laboral and inititally funded by the Caja Laboral, but it is constituted as a second degree co-operative. Its corporate members are the co-operatives which have a potential use for its work and are willing to subsidise it to some extent as an investment in future winners. But IKERLAN also derives an income from contract work for customers outside the Group. The Basque government helps by sponsoring some of the work and by paying thirty of the graduate staff (who are therefore not worker-members). The principal fields of research are electronics, computer technology, and robotics. After seven years' work the robotics research has led to its first practical application: the co-operative DANOBAT introduced the first Spanish-designed robot to the market in 1985. In the same year the quality of IKERLAN's work was aknowledged by the European Community when it was considered for inclusion in the high technology programme Eureka.

The management training school IKASBIDE

This most recent of the Group's educational initiatives has three objectives: first, to ensure the supply of future managers, which is nowadays expected to come mainly from graduate entrants; second, to provide in-service training for working managers; and third, to help rank-and-file members elected to the various councils and boards of management to equip themselves to make decisions about matters that have become complex and highly technical. The school was opened in November 1984.

The main incentive was the realisation, on taking stock of the effects of the recession and in the course of the debate about the future structure of the Group, that there were potential weaknesses in management. Professionalism and quality of management has always been a major factor in the Group's formula for success, but not enough people with the right qualifications seemed to be coming up from within the Group and it had been necessary to recruit outsiders to senior management posts and to pay them, on a consultancy basis, more than they would get as co-operative members. So it was decided to recruit new graduates to a training course specially designed for future managers of co-operatives; those selected would be awarded bursaries, and there would be no contractual commitment for them to join a co-operative, or to be

offered membership, when they completed the course. There were 1500 applicants for the 105 places on the first two-year course which started in January 1985.

The technical subjects covered by the course are what any business school would be expected to teach company-sponsored students: administration and finance, sales and marketing, production control, and general management, and it also covers some technical aspects of co-operative management. But, true to tradition, the in-house course has a more practical slant: it is a sandwich course with an eight-month spell of work experience in one of the industrial co-operatives, and it generally aims to introduce the students to the 'Mondragón Co-operative Experience'.

7 Mondragón in perspective

The fruits of their labour

Co-operatives have their roots in the early nineteenth century when society was being radically transformed by new methods of production. In the old world of farms and craft enterprises relations between master and servant, shopkeeper and customer, were regulated by tradition. People knew each other, farmers and craftsmen had personal obligations to their hired hands. In the new industrial world of large factories and rows of terraced houses relations with shopkeepers were more often impersonal and employers regarded labour as a commodity. The pioneers of the co-operative movement had an answer to this unhealthy development: let the shops be owned and democratically controlled by their customers, and the factories by their workers.

The first part of this prescription proved easier to put into practice than the second. Consumer co-operative societies sprang up all over the world and until recently at least they flourished. The second part did not strike the same response because membership of a worker co-operative is much more demanding. A consumer co-operative merely asks for a little customer loyalty when it fails to offer its members better value than privately owned shops. A worker co-operative on the Mondragón model asks its members to take the not inconsiderable risk of investing their labour and their savings in the same enterprise. It also asks them to subordinate their personal ambitions to the collective greater good.

It is well known that consumer co-operatives originated in Britain: the first co-operatives store was started by the Society of Equitable Pioneers in Toad Lane, Rochdale, in 1844. It is not so well known that it was the pioneers' intention to earn a surplus from the store and to use it to promote production co-operatives. They did indeed launch a textile mill, the Rochdale Co-operative Manufacturing Society, in 1854, but this fell victim to its own success: it put shares on the market to raise money for expansion and was bought up by outsiders. By the turn of the century there were about a hundred worker co-operatives in Britain, but they were the poor relations of the movement. They were outnumbered by the consumer co-operatives, and at a congress in the 1880s a proposal that these should give membership rights and shareholdings to their own employees was rejected. It was left to Mondragón's EROSKI to create, many years later, a joint co-operative of consumers and workers.

The co-operative movement, the trade unions and the socialist parties were built on a common ideological foundation — workers' solidarity against exploitation. In earlier times philosophers argued about man's right to the fruits of his labour — as against that of his landlord or master — but the question remained unresolved. During the industrial revolution this was of little practical significance. It was widely felt, certainly by the workers themselves, that they were not getting their due if the factory owner barely kept them from starvation and creamed off the rest. A political solution in the shape of a socialist state controlled by the workers was a distant prospect. The trade unions' remedy, confrontation, was costly and often unsuccessful. In an unjust world, co-operatives offered a way creating a better society there and then, if only on a smaller scale.

To be fair, it was not only the workers themselves who saw the need for reforms. There were philanthropists in the establishment, and in time legislation was introduced against the worst abuses in the factories. But legislation could be regarded as a threat to the established order, and worker co-operatives were therefore more readily acceptable to the owners of capital — who could even set them up themselves as experiments in social innovation. The most famous of the enlightened capitalists, Robert Owen, owner of textile mills at New Lanark, demonstrated that looking after his workers' welfare was compatible with the accumulation of wealth. He was an

advocate of consumer co-operatives, and as such he is regarded as a father figure by the movement. But later in life he also took an interest in worker co-operatives, which he regarded as a way of protecting the craftsman's way of life against the factory system; however, all his co-operative experiments, both in Britain and at New Harmony and elsewhere in the United States, ended in failure.

The idea was also taken up by the liberal economists of the day. The nineteenth century liberals were of course advocates of the competitive market system, and they would naturally associate control of a business with ownership, but they were uneasy about the concentration of power in the hands of the capitalist. John Stuart Mill, in his later years, became an advocate of what he called 'associations of labourers' that were in effect worker co-operatives.

The British co-operatives have to some extent guarded their independence within the wider labour movement. As early as the 1880s they saw a need for some kind of political representation of their own, and in 1917 they formed the Co-operative Party; but this was affiliated to the Labour Party and elected its own Members of Parliament by agreement; nowadays it merely sponsors Labour candidates.

The trade unions, which play such an important part in the running of the Labour Party, have reservations about worker co-operatives, but since the co-operative movement has always been dominated by the retail side, this has not in the past caused any great problems.

In the mid-1970s, worker co-operatives became a more important issue — and lost credibility — as a result of the ill-fated attempts by Mr Tony Benn, the Labour government's Secretary of State for Industry, to rescue failing companies. Aided by government grants and loans, the Triumph Company at Meriden, the Scottish Daily News in Glasgow, and Kirby Manufacturing and Engineering on Merseyside were relaunched as worker co-operatives; only Triumph, Britain's last remaining motor cycle maker, survived for a while and attracted some public sympathy, but all three failed in the end. It is arguable that these enterprises were not really co-operatives: they were financed by the government and controlled by the trade unions. But by calling them thus, Mr Benn defined Labour's attitude to worker co-operatives: they were a desirable development, provided they were collectively rather than individually owned. The Co-operative Development Agency was set up, in 1978, by a Labour government; but a Labour Party discussion document published in 1980 devotes just sixteen lines to Mondragón, with the conclusion that the model fits the preferred definition of co-operatives but is unacceptable because of the emphasis on individual ownership. In the same year, however, a deputation from the Welsh Trades Union Congress came away with a much more favourable view, and a Labour Party pamphlet published in 1983 treats Mondragón at greater length and with much more sympathy. In recent years, moreover, worker co-operatives have been very actively promoted by the Greater London Enterprise Board, set up by the former Greater London Council to create employment and at the same time to meet certain other social objectives. Like the Caja Laboral, the Greater London Enterprise Board has provided loan finance for its co-operatives, but it is open to doubt whether it has subjected them to the same careful scrutiny and control as the Caja Laboral, and it remains to be seen whether many of the London co-operatives will turn out to be commercially viable.

There can be little doubt that the British labour movement's attitude to worker co-operatives has been influenced by the Mondragón experience, and so, perhaps, has the attitude of people with other political philosophies. The Co-operative Development Agency, at any rate, has been given a new lease of life by the Conservatives.

Though its declared objectives are materialistic and rational, the labour movement is held together by strong emotional bonds which go back to the early days of struggle. Solidarity, essential if the objectives were ever to be attained, was a kind of religion. In Britain, the emotional attachment to the labour movement co-existed comfortably with the Christian religion. A Christian socialist movement was founded as early as 1848 by two Anglican clergymen, Frederick Maurice and Charles Kingsley, together with John Malcolm Ludlow who eventually became Registrar of Co-operatives and Provident Societies. But the majority of working people, if they were practising Christians, belonged to the non-conformist chapels rather than to the established church. It is no accident that printers' and journalists' trade unions call their branches chapels. While religion thus mirrored and perhaps reinforced the class structure, it also helped to hold society together.

On the continent the socialist labour movement and the churches are generally in opposing camps, but with quite different effects on

the structure of workers' institutions in different countries. In Italy, which has by far the largest number of worker co-operatives, they are split on political lines. The original grouping, the *Lega*, has been linked with the Communist Party since the end of the First World War; at that time, the co-operatives close to the Catholic Church split off to form the *Confederazione*; and after the Second World War, those with liberal and social democratic leanings set up the *Associazione*. All three groupings get some preferential treatment when tendering for public works contracts. A hundred years old in 1986, the *Lega* remains the largest and most dynamic of the three.

In France, which has the next largest number of worker co-operatives, they are also strongly represented in the construction sector, and they get some preferential treatment. But in contrast to Italy they have a single organisation, established for over a century, the *Confédération Générale des Sociétés Cooperatives Ouvrières de Production*. The early co-operatives were called *entreprises ouvrières* to distinguish them from *entreprises patronales* belonging to the employers.

In the Federal Republic of Germany there are practically no worker co-operatives unless one counts the very small 'alternative' enterprises. Co-operatives did exist at the turn of the century and again in the crisis years after the First World War. The Hitler régime destroyed the labour movement and all that went with it, and when it was built up again after the Second World War it moved in a new direction — it campaigned for labour legislation that gave workers a significant share in the control of the company that employed them. It is an irony of history that co-determination — *Mitbestimmung* — was introduced in the coal, iron and steel — *Montan* — industries under the auspices of the Allies' military government in order to dissuade the trade unions from pressing for that other form of common ownership, nationalisation; and as it has since turned out, nationalised industries behave very much like private employers in their industrial relations. The coal and steel model of co-determination was later extended in a modified form to all except very small enterprises. It gives the whole workforce the right to elect a works council, and this in turn elects half the members of the company's supervisory board — *Aufsichtsrat* — which has overall strategic control and appoints the executive board — *Vorstand* — which has day-to-day control. In large companies each major division has its works council, and these councils elect a central council which sends members to the *Aufsichtsrat*. The Co-operative Congress in the new organisation of the Mondragón Group is not altogether dissimilar from a German *Aufsichtsrat*, except of course that half the *Aufsichtsrat* members, including the chairman, are elected by the shareholders. Nevertheless, the powers enjoyed by the workforce under this system are considerable — and perhaps sufficient to destroy the desire to own the enterprise.

Spain at the time of the Civil War was deeply divided. The labour movement was associated with the Republic and suppressed by the Franco régime. The Republic was anti-clerical and the Church backed Franco. It is at first sight highly surprising that a family of worker co-operatives was created in these circumstances under the leadership of a Catholic priest. But in the Basque country, Republican territory taken by Franco in 1937, things were different: people regarded themselves as Basque rather than Spanish, the régime suppressed their language and culture and did little to restore the economy of the region, and the Church was the only institution through which they could express their aspirations. Political initiatives in the direction of socialism and trade unionism were quite out of the question in Spain at that time, and the leading role could easily fall to a priest if he was Basque and in tune with the community's needs. The Catholic Church is of course also concerned with the problems of industrial society, and it has a tradition of liberal thought expressed in passages in Papal Encyclicals going back to the nineteenth century; in 1931 Pope Pius XI had referred to the need for the wage contract to be modified by a contract of partnership. The Church did not question the moral value of individual ownership, but it did allow the notion that industrial wealth creation was the product of collective as well as individual effort. Don José María Arizmendiarrieta belonged to this progressive school of Catholic thought and he was closely involved with industry since he had been given the task of teaching Catholic social doctrines to young working people in Mondragón. He had also studied and was keen on the ideas of Robert Owen; he believed that working people should be trusted as mature human beings, and that they should therefore have a say in the running of the enterprise and a share in the profits; so the co-operative idea fitted in very neatly with his ideals. Co-operatives also fitted in with the constraints of the time — they were permitted under legislation designed mainly for agricultural co-operatives which had no political affiliation. It may have helped that many workers in Mondragón came from farming families and were therefore used to the idea of running their own business. But on the whole it seemed that Don José María's Basque Christian social ideology filled the gap left by the eclipse of the traditional labour movement and was as much concerned with the improvement of working and living conditions as with the ownership of the enterprise.

Patterns of ownership

Ownership and control by its workers are of course the key factors that make an enterprise a co-operative. Ownership can take a variety of forms depending on whether:-
- only those who work for the enterprise are owner-members
- all those who work for the enterprise are owner-members
- members hold individual shares in the enterprise (or own it collectively)
- each member has one equal vote (or votes according to the number of shares held)
- the structure of elected councils allows effective membership control.

Provided that the workers retain control, ownership of a co-operative need not be exclusively in their hands. But the lesson was learnt very early in Rochdale that control can pass to outsiders unless there are strict rules about who may own shares in a co-operative; even if members hold individual shares as their title to earnings they cannot be allowed to dispose of them as they wish. The usual rule is that if members leave, their shares are bought back by the co-operative. This creates a problem if a significant number of members leave at the same time, because too much capital might then be withdrawn; this can happen even if the co-operative prospers, since a relatively large number of members may reach retirement age at the same time. There is therefore a provision in Basque co-operative law — and in that of France and other countries too — under which workers who leave a co-operative may keep their investment in it in the form of non-voting shares. The problem has not arisen in the Mondragón co-operatives so far, since few people have retired; but there must be other ways of keeping their capital in the Group through the Caja Laboral, and it may be that exclusive worker-ownership can be maintained.

Mondragón is in this way totally different from companies that offer a small proportion of their ordinary shares to their employees in order to interest them in the problems of the business. The employees have much less at stake in such companies, and they can dispose of the shares. Nevertheless, the schemes originally introduced by progressive employers did help to generate a spirit of participation, and employee share ownership has come to be viewed with favour by governments and encouraged through tax concessions. So far, at least in Britain, these concessions have usually been insufficient to enable employers to acquire a controlling interest by using them.

However the position in the United States is notably different. The American legislation which covers employee share ownership has been designed, among other things, to make full blooded employee buy-outs entirely possible. As a result there are now not less that five hundred substantial businesses in the US in which the employees, often in combination with an employee trust, own either 100% or a controlling interest in the equity. Typical cases include former family businesses where the former owners have preferred to sell to their employees rather than to third parties. They also include the former subsidiaries of large quoted companies. In this latter category the most famous case is the Weirton Steel Corporation in West Virginia. It now employs more that 8500 people, produces more that 2M tons of steel annually and has been consistently profitable since being the subject of an employee buy-out in January 1984.

In America the legislation which has made these developments possible now attracts strong cross party support. There have lately been signs that a similar political consensus is beginning to emerge in Britain. There is no reason, in principle, why legislation similar to that in the US should not be introduced in this country. Equally there is no reason in principle why, if it is introduced, subsequent British experience should differ from that of the United States.

As it is, even without the enabling legislation which has been enacted in the United States, a form of enterprise has developed in Britain which is more like than unlike the Weirton Steel Corporation and is now of considerable and potentially growing importance. This is a form of enterprise in which the share capital is held, in whole or in substantial part, on behalf of its employees by an employee trust.

Businesses of this kind may or may not be able to create the total involvement which comes from employees having, as at Mondragón, a substantial capital stake which may be lost. But they are like co-operatives in that all the earnings accrue to the employees, and, depending on its detailed constitution, it may be controlled by the employees through their elected representatives. This right to a voice in the control of the enterprise without a financial stake in it is in some ways similar to co-determination in German industry. It is in the nature of this kind of enterprise that it almost invariably starts as business built up and owned by an individual or a family, who clearly have a great deal of influence over the new form of the enterprise when it is made over to the employee trust. The largest business of this kind is the John Lewis chain of department stores, which employs some thirty thousand people who are all called partners; the Partnership's constitution provides that the chief executive can be dismissed by a two-thirds majority of the partners' representatives — but since the business is successful, the case has not arisen. The Baxi Partnership, which has about one thousand partners, is similar: the equity is controlled by trustees, but there is an elected partnership council with substantial powers, and there is an employees' share ownership scheme as well. A third well known case is the Scott Bader Commonwealth, which still has a member of the Bader family as chairman, but which has representatives of the elected community council as directors; the company must plough back at least 60%. Up to 50% of the balance may be distributed to the workforce in cash provided that an equal sum is given to charity.

Quite another consideration is whether all the workers employed by a co-operative need be members. There is clearly an advantage in employing non-members on a temporary basis in times of exceptional demand so that the membership is not increased beyond the level that can be sustained when the boom subsides. There is also danger that non-members will feel they are second-class citizens and that shop floor relations will be less than harmonious. But the practice is quite normal and apparently satisfactory in the building industry — the *Lega* co-operatives in Italy have as many non-member employees as members. A divided workforce is also the natural result of a management buy-out. A variant on this is the National Freight Consortium in Britain which was formed as a buy-out of a majority of the shares by a large number of employees, their immediate families, and pensioners; this hybrid between a limited company and a co-operative has been highly successful, but it has a problem in devising workable rules for the disposability of shares and an equitable system for allocating votes to different kinds of shareholders. At Mondragón a few essential specialists have been engaged on contract because the co-operatives failed to attract them as members on normal terms; and ULGOR's after-sales service staff split off from the co-operative to do the work as freelance agents; but the Group has managed to avoid employing non-members as temporary labour.

With regard to individual and collective ownership, the possibilities range from the professional partnership which shares little more than an office to a kibbutz which shares everything. Ownership of a co-operative is never wholly individual because there must be restrictions on the disposal of shares to prevent dilution of the membership. Under British law shares in co-operative societies may normally be bought back only at their nominal value, but the residual assets may be distributed if the co-operative goes into liquidation; the French and Italian laws do not even then allow the distribution of residual assets to the members — they go to a charity. The British industrial common ownership enterprises are not actually owned by the employees, so all their rights are held collectively and they are not in any circumstances entitled to a distribution of capital. Professional partnerships, of lawyers for instance, represent the other extreme: partners buy a share when they join, and when they leave they take with them their share of the partnership's worth at the time.

Mondragón is near the middle of the spectrum as far as the allocation and distribution of funds is concerned: the co-operatives' constitutions require them to put substantial parts of their income to collective reserves, and part of the members' initial capital stake is not returnable. To the members, however, the individual shares must matter most. It will have been an event in their life to have scraped together the *aportatión*, and with any luck they will have seen it grow into a substantial sum for their eventual retirement. Interest payments, though low, are a constant reminder of the size of the stake. Up to seventy percent of any profits may be distributed — though in proportion to wages (*ánticipos*) rather than to the capital stake. The leadership may have to put stress on solidarity, but the Group is certainly not a predominantly collective enterprise.

Originally, when they elected their controlling bodies, members of the Mondragón co-operatives had votes proportionate to their individual shares. This has long since been changed and all members now have equal votes. How much weight these votes carry depends not only on the franchise but on the structure of the system of elected councils. Members have a great deal of say in their own co-operative, at least if it is small, but they have much less control over the Group's central management. This must have been in the minds of the designers of the new Group organisation; there is now substantial delegation to local sub-groups which can be in closer touch with the membership.

How big is beautiful?

It had been the founders' vision that a substantial network of co-operatives would unite the working communities of the Basque country. Something like it has been achieved. How much further can one expect to go? No organisation could sustain the explosive growth of the first decade; the steady growth of the second decade, halted by the recession, has been resumed, but since industry has generally become less labour intensive, it may be unrealistic to expect that the Mondragón Group's membership will rise much above twenty thousand in the foreseeable future. How does this compare with the worker co-operative movements elsewhere?

The national totals are of course different in kind from the Mondragón totals, because there is nowhere a comparable centrally managed group. The data in the table must be treated with caution in other respects as well. For example Britain's 1300 odd co-operatives consist in large part of very small and often 'alternative' ventures. Beyond the name 'co-operative' they have almost nothing in common with their Mondragón counterparts. It is also necessary to emphasise that the British figures exclude those for the John Lewis and Baxi Partnerships and for the National Freight Consortium. These three businesses together employ more than twice the numbers shown in the table. Nevertheless if we focus narrowly on businesses which call themselves co-operatives then it is probably safe to draw one major conclusion from the table — most of them are quite small.

Table 7.1   Worker Co-operatives in some European countries

	Number	Membership
Mondragón	111	19,200
Britain	1,300	20,000
France		
small	689	3,970
10-50 workers	610	13,180
large	126	19,450
Total	1,425	36,600
Italy		
Lega	1,550	80,000
Associazione	1,200	20,000
Confederazione	2,800 (in 1984)	
Total	5,550	125,000

Sources:-
Britain   Co-operative Development Agency, May 1986
France   Confédération Générale des SCOP, June 1986
Italy   John Earle, Rome office of 'The Times', May 1986

The Caja Laboral is not quite like any other bank that may be called 'co-operative'. The Co-operative Bank in Britain, for instance, is not a co-operative in its own right, but a subsidiary of the Co-operative Wholesale Society; although it has branches through-out the country it is comparable with Mondragón. Its balance sheet total in 1985 was 1,227 million (about 250,000 million pesetas compared with Mondragón's 187,000 million). Germany has a large and long-established co-operative banking sector, dominated by the *Raffeisenkassen* and *Volksbanken*, but these institutions are not comparable: their members are the depositors, of whom they have some ten million between them, and their combined assets are of course very much larger than Mondragón's.

The magic of Mondragón

At the end of the first chapter we tried to identify the factors that seemed to have been essential to the Group's success. Having looked in some detail at the evidence we are tempted to highlight five: quality of leadership and management; emphasis on technical competence and training; the commitment which comes from 'the members' capital stakes; the mutual support which the group provides through Lagun Aro and in other ways; and the Caja Laboral Popular.

Mondragón is unique, of course. But the local circumstances which are often cited as an excuse for not attempting to follow the example, were really far from conducive to success: a run-down remote industrial area with no rail or water transport and poor roads; a skilled population used to hardship, yes, but with hardly any technical education; a hostile government. Surely the prospects would have been at least as good in County Durham or the Saarland? The Mondragón movement had leaders who were prepared to devote their lives to building it up without giving much thought to personal financial gain or political acclaim. They had nothing to gain from short-lived success, so they could concentrate on meticulous control of existing ventures and on making sure that their new ventures were really viable. And since their base of operation was the Group's own savings bank, they could avoid the trap of wishful thinking which catches many an entrepreneur who has persuaded someone else to provide funds.

Appendix A: Contract of Association

The standard form of agreement by which an ordinary first degree co-operative becomes an associated co-operative (AC) of the second degree co-operative Caja Laboral Popular (CLP) is set out below in non-legal language. (First degree co-operatives have individual members, second degree co-operatives have other co-operatives and their own employees as members.) This form of agreement, which evolved in the early years of the Mondragón Group's existence, confers all the rights and duties of central management on the CLP; it will have to be modified when the new organisation comes into full effect so that the overall direction of the Group becomes the responsibility of the Co-operative Congress and the Council of Groups.

It is understood that the first degree co-operative has the following standard set of decision-making bodies:-

- General Assembly: All members of the co-operative; has the ultimate responsibility for everything.
- Board of Directors — *Junta Rectora*: Elected by the General Assembly; given delegated powers to make the major decisions and appoint managers (somewhat like the German *Aufsichtsrat*).
- Management — *Gerencia*: Has day-to-day control of the enterprise as in any ordinary company.
- Works council — *Consejo Social*: Delegates elected by various constituencies of rank-and-file members to negotiate with management about matters such as working conditions, health and safety, job grading (somewhat like a joint shop stewards committee, more like the German *Betriebsrat*); the works council also looks after money contributed by the AC to local community activities.

The CLP itself has a similar set of decision-making bodies, except that its General Assembly has comparatively few representatives of its own employees and consists mainly of members of and elected by the ACs.

The CLP also provides a comprehensive set of rules for the organisation of subgroups of ACs. Subgroups for mutual support in a geographical region have existed since ULARCO was formed in 1965, but they will become more important under the new organisation and all ACs will have to belong. Subgroups may be formed on a business area rather than a geographical basis. Subgroups are voluntary associations of ACs similar to second-degree co-operatives without the company status in law (but which they could assume if they wished). Subgroups also have general assemblies made up of delegates from the ACs; their boards and managements remain members of one or other of the constituent ACs. Profits are partly pooled so that loss-making ACs can be subsidised if necessary. If an AC cannot maintain all its members, every effort must be made to transfer them within the subgroup before calling for help from the Group as a whole. The subgroup must try to generate growth and to set up new co-operatives in its area.

Rules

The rights and obligations under this Agreement are set out in the Statutes and Internal Procedures of the CLP. Changes in the relationship between the CLP and the AC may be required by law; they may also be made by a decision of the CLP's General Assembly provided that any changes that may affect the AC have first been submitted to its own representatives.

The AC undertakes to be represented at the CLP's General Assembly. Resolutions passed by this assembly are binding even if the AC was not represented at the time or voted against them. The CLP will send a non-voting observer to the AC's General Assembly if asked to do so by the AC's Board, management, or any 10% of the membership.

Capital and third part guarantees

The AC agrees in principle to assign to the CLP an amount of capital calculated each year by the CLP and approved by its General Assembly. The total provided by all the ACs shall not be more than the CLP needs as capital backing to comply with the Bank of Spain's requirements, and every effort will be made to ensure that no one AC's share will increase by more than 20% from one year to the next.

In addition, third party liability towards the CLP's creditors is accepted by the AC to the limit of 25% of its members' individual capital shares (but no part of its collective reserves).

Finance and audit

The AC will provide the CLP with copies of its annual accounts and of its budget for the following year in the form laid down by the CLP; the AC will also provide certain financial data monthly. In return, the

CLP will provide the AC with regular reports on its own financial planning and other economic and technical matters that may be of interest. The information will be treated as strictly confidential by both parties, especially if disclosure could harm the co-operatives' image.

The AC agrees to an audit by the CLP's audit department at least once in four years; the audit department will then produce a report on the AC's economic, social and business development with recommendations about existing or potential problems. The CLP has the right to carry out additional audits if in its view there are special circumstances that warrant it; an additional audit at the AC's own expense may be requested by its General Assembly, management, or any 10% of the membership.

To finance its operations the AC will be able to borrow from the CLP on credit terms in line with the CLP's general regulations, and the AC will bank any spare monies with the CLP, on the understanding that all business will be carried out in a spirit of mutual co-operation.

The AC will respect the principle of Group loyalty and mutual assistance in its production plans, personnel selection, placing of orders and in any other business matters, as long as this does not interfere with its own interests and autonomy.

Co-operative principles
- Open door: Membership is voluntary and open to all who can be of use and will accept the responsibilities.
- All workers must be members: Other workers may be hired only in exceptional circumstances and the number must not exceed 5% of the membership.
- Democracy: The organisation will be run by people who have been elected by and are accountable to the members, or who have been appointed according to rules made by the members.
- Community funds: the AC must have collectively owned funds: reserves for investment in expansion so that more workers can be brought into the co-operative sector; and a Social Fund devoted to co-operative projects of benefit to the community rather than only the AC's members.
- Limited individual profit-sharing: Members' capital earns only a fixed rate of interest; additional income is split between individual and collective holdings.

- Co-operative spirit: The AC's membership must give positive proof of respect for the governing and executive bodies, carry out their duties efficiently, and obey the co-operative's rules; working relationships should be flexible; all and especially managerial appointments shall be made on co-operative principles; managers should work to high professional standards; they should demonstrate their social involvement and responsibility, their commitment to the co-operative and their desire to promote and develop it.

Members' shares in capital and profits

- Initial contribution — *aportación*: New members must contribute to the AC's capital an amount fixed by its Assembly within the range of 80% — 120% of the amount fixed by the CLP for its own members. The contribution may be paid in instalments over two years (or up to the age of 20 by members who are under 18 when they join). This contribution cannot be withdrawn until the member leaves or retires; up to 25% may be put into the collective reserve which is not returned at all.
- Interest: Members' individual shares of the capital earn interest at a rate laid down by the AC's General Assembly at not more that 3% above the Bank of Spain's base rate. If the AC's financial position permits, up to 6% interest may be drawn in cash.
- Distribution of profits: The income attributable to the AC's members when all expenses have been met is divided as follows:-

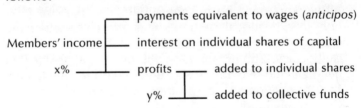

x = profits as a percentage of members' total income
y = percentage of profits added to collective funds

The rule is that y shall be at least 30, and that if x is greater than 30, y shall equal x. Thus the larger the profit relative to the basic income, the more of it goes to collective funds. When there are losses, not more than 30% may be covered from collective funds.

At least 10% of the profit must go the the Social Fund to be used for the benefit of the community and not exclusively for that of the ACs members.
- Withdrawals of capital: members may take out up to 25% of their share of the annual profit, but only when the co-operative's performance has met certain conditions: collective reserves must cover the fixed assets plus half the working capital, less than one-third of the total capital should be represented by loans, members' individual shares must cover the average cost per job, and the admission of new members must not be limited by lack of resources.
- Revaluation of individual shares: members' individual capital shares may be increased annually to compensate for inflation, but by no more than calculated from the National Statistical Institute's index chosen by the CLP for the revaluation of fixed assets.

Wages structure
All jobs in the AC will be graded on a scale from 1.0 to 3.0 in units of 0.1 according to the norms applied by the other ACs in the Group as set out in the evaluation manual compiled by the CLP. Advance payments equivalent to wages (*anticipos*) and individual shares of profits alike will be proportional to the grade, but the advance payments may be increased by up to 50% in recognition of hours worked and other special circumstances.

In principle, total advance payments, including social security contributions and bonuses, must not exceed the going rate in the AC's area. In practice the CLP will lay down rates of pay for its own employees, and the ACs will set rates between 95% and 105% of those of CLP employees on the same grade if standard hours are worked, or pro rata if the hours are different; but the AC may pay less than 95% of the CLP rates to avoid making a loss.

Annulment
Grounds for annulment may be serious breaches of the agreement by either side, or simply the AC's decision to quit.

If the CLP decides that the agreement should be annulled its General Assembly must first issue two warnings, and the AC must make these known to its members. The decision must then be ratified by a two-thirds majority at an extraordinary meeting of the

CLP's General Assembly, and the expelled AC will then be given six to twelve months' grace to restructure its finances.

If a co-operative gives up or loses its association with the CLP it is not relieved of the liabilities set out in the CLP's statutes or of its share of third-party guarantees.

Exceptions in the application of the agreement

If an AC finds itself unable to comply with a clause of this agreement it must negotiate a temporary exemption with the CLP and have it approved by the CLP's General Assembly.

Appendix B: Mondragón co-operatives at the end of 1985

The co-operatives' membership fluctuates and their classification may be inaccurate because of changes in the product range. Place names are mostly in Basque, but the Spanish names are used for Mondragón (Basque name Arrasate), Bilbao (Bilbo), San Sebastián (Donostia) and Vitoria (Gasteiz). Provinces are indicated by the letter in brackets after the place name:- A = Alava, G = Guipúzcoa, N = Navarra, V = Vizcaya.

This list does not include the educational and housing co-operatives.

Co-operative	Main product or activity	Location	Founded	Members
Castings, Forgings				
AMAT	pipe fittings	Mondragón (G)	1963	365
AMPO	valves	Idiazabal (G)	1964	246
EDERLAN	castings	Eskoriatza (G)	1963	671
ENARA	valves & fittings	Oñati (G)	1962	210
FUNCOR	agricultural machinery	Elorrio (V)	1956	226
SAKANA	castings	Lacunza (N)	1975	85
TOLSAN	forgings	Amorebieta (V)	1957	126
Machine tools, Machines, Control equipment				
ANEKO	agricultural equipment	Antzuola (G)		11
ARRASATE	steel cutting & forming	Mondragón (G)	1957	342
AURKI	numerical control	Mondragón (G)	1980	231
AURRENAK	foundry moulds & dies	Vitoria (A)	1974	58
BATZ	dies	Igorre (V)	1963	92
BERRIOLA	electrical equipment			93
BIHAR	process controls	Bilbao (V)	1982	18
DANOBAT	machine tools	Elgoibar (G)	1966	490
DOIKI	precision tools & gauges	Mallabia (V)	1972	48
EGURKO	woodworking machines	Zumaya (G)	1969	109
EKAIN	motors	Usurbil (G)	1974	40
FAGOR INDUST.	catering & laundry equipment	Oñati (G)	1973	322
GAIKO				10
GAZTELU	lifting gear & conveyors	Usurbil (G)	1978	45
GOITI	presses	Elgoibar (G)	1962	58
GURIA INDUST	fishing boats	Pasaia	1978	147
GURIA OP	excavators	Irún (G)	1961	249
IRIZAR	coach & truck bodies	Ormaiztegi (G)	1963	328
IZARRAITZ	sawing machines	Azkoitia (G)	1978	83
KENDU	milling cutters	Segura (G)	1976	59
KIDE	frozen food equipment	Ondárroa (V)	1979	45
LATZ	drills	Andoain (G)		48

Worker-owners: Mondragón revisited

LEALDE	lathes	Lekeitio (V)	1974	57
MATRICI	dies for pressings	Zamudio (V)	1963	323
MATRIPLAST	moulds for plastics	Zamudio (V)		47
OCHANDIANO T	workshops			59
OINAKAR		Oñati (G)		22
ONA-PRES	hydraulic presses	Valle de Trápaga(V)	1978	81
ORTZA	wood saws	Huarte-Pamplona (N)	1982	37
SCOINER	garbage grinders	Hernani (G)	1982	8
SORALUCE	drilling machines	Bergara (G)	1961	177
TXURTXIL	grinding machines	Bergara (G)	1978	56
UROLA	plastics moulding machines	Legazpia (G)	1980	146
ZUBIOLA	woodworking machines	Azpeitia (G)	1967	35

Components, Materials, Packaging

ALECOOP	testing equipment	Mondragón (G)	1966	311
ALKARGO	transformers, motors	Mungia (V)	1965	98
ALTTUR	pumps	Ordizia (G)	1982	26
BERTAKO	cardboard packages	Pamplona (N)	1974	69
BIURRARENA	machinery services	San Sebastián (G)	1967	9
CIKAUTXO	rubber mouldings	Berriatúa (V)	1971	186
COINALDE	wire products, nails	Vitoria (A)	1965	33
COPRECI	domestic appliance parts	Aretxabaleta (G)	1963	1015
DANONA LIT	brochures, books	Oyarzun (G)	1978	51
EDERFIL	electric wire	Legorreta (G)	1976	48
EIKA	domestic heating elements	Markina (V)	1973	156
ELKAR	catalogues, booklets	Bilbao (V)	1967	38
EMBEGA	decorative metal panels	Estella (N)	1971	98
FAGOR ELECTRO	electronics	Mondragón (G)	1966	528
GAIKO	boilers	Alsasua (N)	1974	10
GOIZPER	brakes & clutches	Antzuola (G)	1961	129
HERTELL	pumps	Ikaztegieta (G)	1979	14
IMPRECI	gears, car parts	Bergara (G)	1962	129
LEUNKOR	machining	Mondragón (G)	1982	57
MAIER	plastics injection	Gernika (V)	1973	154
MATZ-ERREKA	nuts & bolts	Bergara (G)	1973	79
OIARSO	medical equipment	Oyarzun (G)	1981	33
ORKLI	gas appliances	Ordizia (G)	1982	206
OSATU	medical electrical instrum.	Bérriz (V)	1982	816
RPK	springs, coils	Vitoria (A)	1974	74
TAJO	injection moulds & parts	Oyarzun (G)	1963	223
ZERTAN	switches	Estella (N)	1978	180

Consumer durables

BASARTE	upholstered furniture	Azkoitia (G)	1980	25
COINMA	home & office furniture	Vitoria (A)	1964	55
DANONA	furniture	Azpeitia (G)	1962	410
DIKAR	hobbies & toys	Bergara (G)	1978	75
DORMICOOP	bedroom	furniture Elgeta (G)	1959	40
EREDU	camping & leisure furniture	Legorreta (G)	1963	40
FAGOR CLIMA	water heaters	Mondragón (G)	1982	205
GOGAR	loudspeakers	Urretxu (G)	1981	12
GUROLA	classical bedroom furniture	Azpeitia (G)	1968	86
HERRIOLA	lighting systems	Murelaga (V)	1982	41

Appendix B: Mondragón co-operatives at the end of 1985

IKUS XXI	spectacle frames	Zarautz (G)	1983	21
LAN-MOBEL	furniture	Azpeitia (G)		125
LENNIZ	kitchen furniture	Oñati (G)	1981	121
LEROA	furniture	Azpeitia (G)		22
MAIAK	dining-room tables	Azpeitia (G)	1980	51
MUNKO	electric appliances	Mungia (V)	1982	42
OIHANA	tables & chairs	Espinal (N)	1982	25
ORBEA	bicycles	Mallabia (V)	1969	194
RADAR	pressure cookers	Eskoriatza (G)	1979	120
ULGOR	white goods	Mondragón (G)	1956	2256
URALDI	bathroom fittings	Gernika (V)	1982	37

Construction

COVIMAR	stone facings	Amorebieta (V)	1965	82
ORONA	lifts & hoists	Hernani (G)	1964	410
ULMA	machinery	Oñati (G)	1962	494
URSSA	steel construction	Vitoria (A)	1961	256
VICON	buildings	San Sebastián (G)	1960	80

Food and agriculture

ARTXA		Vitoria (V)		2
BARREBETXE	hothouse vegetables	Markina (V)	1980	22·
BEHI-ALDE	milk	Olaeta Aramayona(A)	1978	26·
COSECHEROS AL		Laguardia (A)	1982	1
ETORKI		Llodio (A)		35
IAN	canned vegetables	Villafranca (N)	1974	51
LANA	timber	Oñati (G)	1976	132
MIBA	animal feeds, farm supplies	Markina (V)	1963	10

Retail stores

EROSKI		Elorrio (V)	1969	1348

Services

AUZO-LAGUN	catering & cleaning	Mondragon (G)	1977	275
ONDOAN	planning consultants	Bilbao (V)	1981	21
ULDATA	data processing	Mondragón (G)	1982	62
ULMATIK				64

Total membership of the Commercial Area co-operatives (31 Dec 85)   17054

Financial area

CAJA LABORAL POPULAR		Mondragón (G)		
LAGUN-ARO	health, pensions etc	,,	1969	40
SEGUROS L-A	insurance	,,	1982	20
LAGUN-EXPORT	export agency	,,		
IKASBIDE	management training school	,,		
IKERLAN	research centre	,,		

Source: Caja Laboral Popular